The Photographers' Guide to Photoshop v.4

Produced by *Digital SLR Photography* at:
6 Swan Court, Cygnet Park,
Peterborough, Cambs PE7 8GX
Phone: 01733 567401. Fax 01733 352650
Email: enquiries@digitalslrphoto.com
Online: www.digitalslrphoto.com

Editorial

To contact editorial phone: 01733 567401
Editor **Daniel Lezano**
daniel_lezano@dennis.co.uk
Art Editor **Luke Marsh**
luke_marsh@dennis.co.uk
Features Editor **Caroline Wilkinson**
caroline_wilkinson@dennis.co.uk
Features Writer **Jordan Butters**
jordan_butters@dennis.co.uk
Designer **Luke Medler**
luke_medler@dennis.co.uk
Editorial Co-ordinator **Jo Lezano**
jo_lezano@dennis.co.uk
Editorial contributors:
Fay Bacon, Amy Dresser, Helen Dixon, Lee Frost,
Chanelle Segerius-Bruce and Donna Willingham

Advertising & Production

Display & Classified Sales: 020 7907 6651
Advertising Sales **Guy Scott-Wilson**
guy_scott-wilson@dennis.co.uk
Sales Executive **Peter Smith**
peter_smith@dennis.co.uk
Production Controller **Daniel Stark**
daniel_stark@dennis.co.uk
Digital Production Manager **Nicky Baker**
nicky_baker@dennis.co.uk

Management

MAGBOOK PUBLISHER **DHARMESH MISTRY**
OPERATIONS DIRECTOR **ROBIN RYAN**
MD OF ADVERTISING **JULIAN LLOYD-EVANS**
NEWSTRADE DIRECTOR **DAVID BARKER**
COMMERCIAL & RETAIL DIRECTOR **MARTIN BELSON**
PUBLISHING DIRECTOR **JOHN GAREWAL**
CHIEF OPERATING OFFICER **BRETT REYNOLDS**
GROUP FINANCE DIRECTOR **IAN LEGGETT**
CHIEF EXECUTIVE **JAMES TYE**
CHAIRMAN **FELIX DENNIS**

Welcome...

"The very best photographers have always been those with skills in capturing pictures with their camera and producing great results in post-production. In the past, this was by using film, which was processed and printed in the darkroom, today it's by shooting digitally and manipulating images on the computer, usually using Photoshop as the software of choice. Regardless of the type of digital camera you use, once you have your images on your PC or Mac, Photoshop allows you to experiment, enhance and manipulate to your heart's content. Whether using Adobe's affordable Photoshop Elements package or the more powerful Creative Suite, there are countless ways to improve or transform your photographs. Of course, such a sophisticated tool requires time and effort to master, which is where *The Photographers' Guide to Photoshop* will help. Produced by photographers for photographers, this guide is the perfect introduction to Photoshop, guiding you through the key features and tools that you need to use, as well as providing you with a variety of techniques geared towards helping you make the most of your digital images. By following the jargon-free advice given by our team of experts, you can look forward to mastering key Photoshop techniques, while having fun as you learn new skills along the way. We've covered various techniques, from basic skills that enhance images to more advanced options that transform them. All the best!"

DANIEL LEZANO, EDITOR

Meet our team of Photoshop experts

All our experts are team members or regular contributors to *Digital SLR Photography* magazine. For more expert advice and inspiration, pick up the latest issue available on the second Tuesday of every month. For further information visit the magazine's website at www.digitalslrphoto.com

CAROLINE WILKINSON
An avid enthusiast photographer for several years, Caroline uses her in-depth knowledge of Photoshop and creative skills in post-production to add extra impact and polish to pictures.

LUKE MARSH
A keen DSLR photographer, Luke's also the creative genius behind the look of *Digital SLR Photography* magazine and this MagBook, as well as a Photoshop expert.

LEE FROST
A professional photographer and writer for two decades, Lee regularly combines his in-camera skills with Photoshop to get the very best from his images. www.leefrost.co.uk

JORDAN BUTTERS
With his roots in shooting motorsport, Jordan's passion for photography has evolved to include Photoshop. He is highly skilled in creating stunning images in post-production.

CONTENTS

24 ADJUSTMENT LAYER

26 BLEND MODES

28 LEVELS

6 Introduction
Welcome to Photoshop and a
wealth of creative opportunities!

10 The fundamentals
Learn how to use the tools at the heart of
Photoshop's success and uncover a few hidden
secrets along the way

12 **CROP TOOL**
14 **SHARPENING**
16 **NOISE**
18 **TRANSFORM**
20 **CLONE STAMP & HEALING BRUSH**
22 **LAYERS & LAYER MASKS**
24 **ADJUSTMENT LAYERS**
26 **LAYER BLEND MODES**
28 **LEVELS & CURVES**
32 **DODGE & BURN**
34 **BLACK & WHITE**
36 **HUE/SATURATION**
38 **SELECTION TOOLS**

46 The Raw essentials
How using Photoshop with Raw
files can improve your photography

46 **INTRODUCTION TO RAW**
50 **HOW TO BATCH PROCESS RAW FILES**
52 **CREATE PERFECT EXPOSURES**
54 **COMBINE RAW FILES**

57 Basic techniques
Top tutorials covering a range of essential
Photoshop techniques

58 **CREATE DRAMATIC BLACK & WHITES**
60 **HOW TO TONE AN IMAGE**
62 **MASTER DUOTONES**
64 **USE SHADOWS & HIGHLIGHTS**
66 **ADD A DIGITAL ND GRAD**
68 **REPLACE A SKY**
70 **STITCH A PANORAMA**
72 **RESTORE OLD PRINTS**
74 **APPLY LENS FLARE**
76 **ADD A VIGNETTE**
78 **TEXTURISE YOUR PHOTOS**
80 **SELECT FINE HAIR FOR COMPOSITING**
82 **ADD MOVEMENT**

84 Portrait Retouching
Learn how to retouch portraits like a pro with
our in-depth advice and advanced tutorials

97 Creative effects
Our top choices for special effects
to get your creative juices flowing

98 **LEARN HOW TO 'COLOUR POP'**
100 **BLUR LANDSCAPES**
102 **CREATE A RETRO PORTRAIT**
104 **PAINT A BLACK & WHITE COLOUR**
106 **TURN PHOTOS INTO SKETCHES**
108 **REPLICATE '80S POP ART**
110 **PAINT A PICTURE**
112 **SHRINK A SCENE**
114 **CREATE A CARICATURE**
116 **MAKE IT RAIN**
118 **MISTY MORNINGS**
120 **GOLDEN HOUR PORTRAIT**
122 **PSEUDO TEN-STOP EFFECT**
124 **CREATE A SILHOUETTE**
126 **TURN DAY TO NIGHT**
128 **TATTOO YOUR SUBJECT**
130 **MANIPULATE SMOKE TRAILS**
132 **PAINT SPLATTER EFFECTS**
134 **CREATE A COMIC BOOK**

137 Presentation ideas
Once you have created a great image, spend
some time on how to present it!

138 **ADD A FRAME & TEXT**
140 **ADD A MODERN GRUNGE FRAME**
142 **CREATE A TRIPTYCH**
144 **CREATE YOUR OWN CHRISTMAS CARDS**

146 Useful shortcuts
A selection of PC and Mac keyboard shortcuts
to help improve your Photoshop workflow

130 MANIPULATE SMOKE TRAILS

DEEP INTO EXTRA TIME, THE BALL FELL TO THE STRIKER...

OOOF!!!

134 CREATE A COMIC BOOK

...GOAL!!

68 REPLACE A SKY

84 PORTRAIT RETOUCHING

138 ADD A FRAME PEBBLES

PHOTOSHOP. THE DIGITAL PHOTOGRAPHERS' CHOICE!

PHOTOGRAPHY IS ABOUT creativity, always has been. Since its inception, photographers haven't simply been content to document their surroundings but have sought to enhance, embellish, beautify and distort their imagery, be it via the darkroom or with in-camera techniques. Photoshop is just another tool in the creative arsenal, though it happens to be a damn good one – the best possible. Everything that was done in the film darkroom can be recreated in Photoshop, and far more besides. Images that are now appearing in this digital age are really pushing the boundaries of the imagination. So if you haven't already jumped on the Photoshop bandwagon, it's really time to take that leap. You're missing out on the chance to really explore your creative self. Even if your ambitions are a little more modest, you'll find that there isn't an image in the world that can't be improved by Photoshop in some manner, even if it's a matter of a simple contrast tweak or basic blemish removal. And the best way to learn is just to get stuck in. After, of course, you've familiarised yourself with the basics in our feature-packed guide to the best imaging software on the planet! Here are our favourite reasons for using Photoshop...

1) Raw conversion: All digital cameras come with their own brand software to help convert Raw files into an editable image state (ie JPEG or TIFF). However, not all are straightforward to use. Photoshop and Photoshop Elements come with their own Raw converter, Adobe Camera Raw (ACR), which just happens to be rather good at the job. Most people tend to plump for the Adobe engine rather than the camera manufacturer's own, not least because of its seamless integration with Photoshop.

2) Exposure control: Photoshop gives you the kind of control over exposure that darkroom enthusiasts could have only dreamed of. Not only can you lighten or darken the image as a whole, but you can work on specific tones, lightening the highlights or darkening shadows, for example. You can also work on specific areas to 'dodge' and 'burn' in the traditional darkroom manner – darkening a sky perhaps, or bringing out a bit more detail in a landscape foreground.

3) Colour control: We're not just talking about warming things up or cooling them down. You can tweak colours in any way imaginable and locally as well as globally, changing the colour of someone's eyes, hair, or perhaps the colour of a particularly bad tie. And you can control colour saturation as well as hue, so you can make those sunsets really burn.

4) Better black and white: Yes, you can shoot black and white in camera but, no, it won't do. First, you'll be shooting JPEG and secondly, all you're doing is performing a basic desaturation, which means you'll be discarding vital information. Anyone who's printed in the traditional darkroom knows there's a bit more to mastering monochrome. Photoshop lets you control specific colour channels in the way that black and white filters did for film cameras.

5) Blemish removal: On a basic level, this means polishing portraits a little by removing spots, moles and wrinkles, but this process can be extended to pretty much anything with the clever combination of Clone Stamp and Healing Brush Tools. You can remove a telegraph pole from an otherwise picture-perfect landscape, an unwanted reflection from a window, and so on.

6) Montage: Layers allow you to montage (otherwise known as composite) different images, in the same way that you might have once cut and pasted family photos. But

Photoshop allows you to go that extra mile. You can change a cloudy sky for a clear one, add trees where there were none, or even place a person in a completely different background scene. This type of montage is also known as compositing and has grown in popularity with amateur users and professionals alike.

7) Subject enhancement: As well as taking out aspects you don't really like and sticking in stuff that wasn't really there, you can also enhance what you've already got. Aside from the colour and exposure controls for whitening teeth or pulling out grey hairs, you could change the shape and size of parts of your image with various Transform commands. And yes, that can mean slimmer hips and bigger biceps, but it could also mean ironing out the converging verticals of a tall building or scaling down a hand that's too close to a wide-angle lens.

8) Web preparation: If you want to post your photos in a forum, an online gallery or your own website, Photoshop is certainly going to come in handy. You can resize them, sharpen them, convert them to sRGB mode and save them with the appropriate JPEG quality setting.

9) Special Effects: Photoshop has a massive array of filters to enable you to achieve special effects. Turn photos into watercolour paintings, add frames and borders, add rain to a cloud scene, the list goes on.

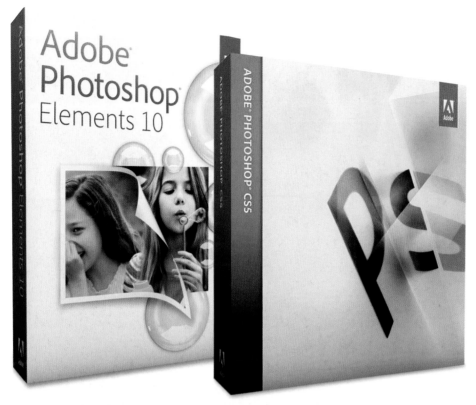

Which Photoshop: Elements or CS?

PHOTOSHOP COMES in two distinct flavours. First, you've got the full-blown Creative Suite professional version, which has run from its first installment back in 1990 all the way to Photoshop 7, then CS, CS2, CS3, CS4 and now CS5 (effectively Photoshop 12). Then there's the cut-down, beginner-friendly, consumer version called Photoshop Elements, now at version 10. To give you an idea of the price difference, you can pick up a copy of Photoshop CS5 for anything between £200 and £600 online, whereas you can get hold of the latest version of Elements for around £60.

Truth be told, unless you're planning complex composites that involve cutting out intricate shapes, you'll be fine with Elements. If you're at the stage where you're good enough to be doing detailed cut-outs, you'll already know what the Pen Tool and the Channels palette are and how to use them and will probably already have access to a copy of Photoshop. You can perform all the basic edits you'll need as a beginner in Elements and a few intermediate edits, especially as Elements 10 now features Layer Masks. As a first-time buyer, the only occasion you might want to plump for the full version is if you plan to use retouching as part of a semi- or fully-professional photographic workflow or have ambitions for advanced retouching. In this case, it's perhaps better to familiarise yourself with Photoshop from the start to save making the transition later on.

While the Elements interface is a little different from that found on Creative Suite, there are enough similarities so that photographers migrating from one to the other won't find it too alien.

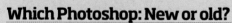

Which Photoshop: New or old?

If you're a first-time buyer, there's little incentive to buy earlier versions of either Photoshop or Photoshop Elements as there appears to be little difference in prices and you have the added compatibility problems with newer digital cameras (for which updates are often only released for the latest versions). Owners of older versions may be forced to upgrade their copies for this reason. If you're not planning to invest in the latest and greatest digital camera and already own a copy of CS, CS2, CS3 or CS4, you'll have to weigh the upgrade price against new features.

It's worth noting that there's certainly nothing spectacular that you couldn't be without in earlier versions – there are plenty of pro retouchers and photographers who refuse to upgrade. Many of the new features are quite gimmicky, though the Photomerge advancements were a big improvement for panoramic enthusiasts in CS3, CS4's Clone Stamp Tool overlay and CS5's Content-Aware Fill function alone make the upgrade worth considering if you do a lot of clean-up work. Also, the addition of Layer Masks in Elements 9 is a big bonus.

File formats

Check out the File Format drop-down list in the Photoshop Save As dialogue and get a shock at the multitude of options available. Panic not, though; there are only really four formats worth discussing.

✓ Photoshop
Photoshop EPS
JPEG
Large Document Format
Photoshop PDF
Photoshop 2.0
Photoshop Raw
Scitex CT
TIFF
Photoshop DCS 1.0
Photoshop DCS 2.0

✓ **PC & Mac shortcuts**
You can use shortcuts for some commands. Most Mac shortcuts use the **Cmd** (Apple) key. Where it's not specified, we've stated Mac shortcuts in the text but if you use a PC, swap the **Cmd** button for **Ctrl**. Both PC & Mac use **Alt** and **Shift** keys, too

RAW

This is the catch-all term given to the different proprietary file formats that come directly out of a digital camera when shooting in Raw (a Canon EOS 5D Mk II Raw file, for example, has the extension .CR2). These files need converting into editable information via a Raw converter, such as Adobe Camera Raw (ACR), which comes packaged with both Photoshop and Elements. Shooting Raw allows access to the full range of information recorded by the camera sensor, giving more room to correct for exposure mistakes and to make edits to your image without chancing visible degradation. Raw files give you access to 16-bits of information, as opposed to a JPEG's 8-bits.

PSD

The PSD file is a Photoshop format that allows all Photoshop information, such as layers and saved selections, to be easily stored and re-accessed at a later date. It's an uncompressed format and maintains the full 16-bits of information. While TIFF files do give you the option of including Photoshop layers, the file size increases disproportionately, making PSD the file format of choice for editing your images. When the image is finally flattened, it can be saved as a TIFF or JPEG, although it's always a good idea to keep the PSD file with all the layers work you've done in case you need to make any additional changes at a later date.

JPEG

The JPEG is a compressed file format, designed to keep file size as low as possible with as little quality loss as possible. It uses what's termed a 'lossy' version of compression, meaning image information is thrown away for good. The amount discarded depends on the compression setting. A JPEG file retains only 8-bits rather than 16-bits of information, making it less useful as a format for image editing; the decrease in available information can produce signs of degradation if adjustments are pushed particularly hard. The reduced file size makes JPEGs great for web reproduction, email and even magazine reproduction, with a quality setting of 9 or more.

TIFF

The TIFF is generally an uncompressed file format (though there is a 'lossless' compression option), and an alternative to the JPEG for distributing images once you've made all your edits in Photoshop and flattened the layers. File sizes are considerably bigger than JPEGs, so it's used as a maximum quality option if you're prepared to distribute images on a CD or upload them via FTP – forget email! Those without a copy of Photoshop are normally able to open a TIFF file without any problems. It can hold 16-bits of information, but as it's not generally used for editing, it's better to convert your images to 8-bits before saving as a TIFF to keep down the file size.

The Toolbar

Photoshop's tools are generally quick and easy to understand as their descriptions usually outline their function well. A small black arrow to the bottom right of a tool icon indicates a sub-menu with further tools accessed by clicking and holding.

 Move Can be used to move pixel information on a layer, text or an active selection. Just click and drag.

 Zoom Click to zoom in, or *Alt* and click to zoom out. You may also choose to use *Ctrl* (PC) or *Cmd* (Mac) plus the **+** or **−** keys.

 Hand Used for moving around your image when zoomed in. Access quickly by holding down the spacebar instead.

 Eyedropper Select a colour from your image by clicking on the areas or hold it down to reveal any of the three tools housed underneath, including Ruler.

 Marquee Use these tools to make a selection based on a shape such as a rectangle or ellipse. Simply drag to size.

 Lasso Draw your own custom selections with this tool, either freehand or using magnetic polygon points.

 Quick Selection Houses both the Quick Selection and Magic Wand Tool for semi-automated selections. Use by adjusting the Tolerance in the Options bar.

 Text Type text directly onto your image using any of the installed fonts. Type horizontally or vertically and create selections based on your type.

 Crop Crop out unwanted aspects from the edges of your image. Set a specific width-to-height ratio if needed in the Options bar.

 Healing Brush Replace blemishes with nearby clean pixel information and have it blend in with surrounding pixels. Also houses the Spot Healing Brush Tool, Patch Tool and Red Eye in CS4/5.

 Clone Stamp Allows you to copy and paste pixels from one area to another without the blending of the Healing Brush.

 Eraser Remove pixel information manually or in a semi-automated manner using the Background or Magic Eraser Tool.

 Brush One of the tools used most often, particularly for painting information in and out of an image when combined with a Layer Mask. You control its Opacity and edge Hardness via the Options bar. The Pencil Tool and Color Replacement Tool sit underneath.

 Gradient Draw gradients directly onto layers or their masks. Also houses the Paint Bucket Tool for single colour fill.

 Blur Soften selected areas of your image or sharpen and smudge them with the two other useful tools housed underneath Blur.

 Shape Draw shapes or lines using any one of the default shapes, or choose another with the Custom Shape Tool.

 Dodge & Burn The Dodge Tool lightens and the Burn Tool darkens depending on the Exposure level set in the Options bar. You can choose whether to focus on Shadows, Mid-tones or Highlights and there's also a Sponge Tool for increasing or decreasing colour saturation.

 History Brush (CS4/5 only) Go back in time by painting previous states into your image in conjunction with the History palette.

 Pen (CS4/5 only) Allows the user to create curved as well as straight-edge selections to accurately outline solid-edge subjects.

 Direct Selection (CS4/5 only) This tool and the one it hides are for selecting and moving paths created with the Pen and Shape Tool.

 Quick Mask Mode (CS4/5 only) View selections as a translucent red mask rather than marching ants. When active, you can paint onto your image with a Black or White brush to add or subtract from the selection. Press *Q* to turn it on and off.

Menus, tools and palettes

THE PHOTOSHOP WORKSPACE can be a daunting place at first, with its vast array of features. However, once you grasp a basic understanding of just a few key areas, you'll be up and running in no time. Here we'll be looking at the workspace of Photoshop Elements and although there are differences between this interface and that of CS3, CS4 or CS5, Adobe does a great job with crossing over packages to encourage a progression for users as they become more experienced. The three key areas to understand are the Toolbar (which runs vertically on the left side and incorporates the Options bar running horizontally above it), the Menu bar (which runs horizontally along the top of the workspace), and, finally, the palettes. All these items can be hidden or made visible via the Window tab, allowing users to customise the workspace to their individual needs.

The Menu bar

EDIT As well as hosting options for general preferences and keyboard shortcuts, the Edit menu is home to Cut, Copy and Paste, though all these are accessed easier via their keyboard shortcuts. The Transform commands are located here, too, allowing you to perform things such as Scale, Rotate and Skew.

IMAGE All the popular image adjustments such as Levels and Curves can be found here, though usually you'll want to add these as Adjustment Layers via the button in the Layers palette, rather than applying them directly to pixel information. The Image menu also lets you alter size via the Image Size command.

LAYER The Layer menu is home to popular layer-based commands like Convert to Smart Object, Merge Layers and Flatten Image, and you can also add Adjustment Layers from here. In truth, virtually everything here is better accessed by keyboard shortcuts or buttons on the Layers palette itself.

SELECT Everything to do with selections is here, such as Select All, Deselect and Select Inverse. You can also modify selections via this menu with commands like Expand, Contract and, most commonly, Feather. This menu also gives access to the very useful Transform Selection and Color Range commands.

FILTER Along with being home to a variety of special-effects filters, the Filters menu also includes two of the most often used filters in Photoshop – Unsharp Mask and Gaussian Blur. These two filters are integral to much of the work done in Photoshop and can be employed for a variety of purposes.

Palettes

There are several interchangeable palettes accessed in the Window tab of the menu including Colour Swatch, Histogram, Info, Navigator, Styles and Effects. Here are two you won't be able to live without...

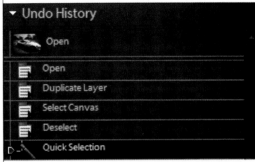

History Everything you do in Photoshop, whether it be applying a brush stroke, filter or deleting a layer, is recorded in the History palette. The number of steps kept in memory is specified in the Preferences palette (the default is 20, but 40 is safer). To go back step by step through your history, click *Cmd+Alt+Z* (Mac) or *Ctrl+Z* for PC users.

Layers This palette contains all your pixel, vector and Adjustment Layers, as well as their masks. You can reorder and delete these layers at any time, organise layers into groups, turn them on and off with the visibility icon and, of course, add Layer Styles from the palette itself. There's also a context menu for more layer commands, such as Flatten Image.

Photo Bin (Elements)

The Photo Bin in Photoshop Elements is an organisational tool that shows thumbnails of all the files you have open in the workspace. Underneath the thumbnail you'll see the file name, and when you click on a thumbnail, that file becomes the active document. A right-click on a thumbnail gets you to a shortcut menu where you can minimise, close or rotate the image, create a duplicate file or access the image's original camera data.

✔ **Customise your space**
The Photoshop interface is fully customisable. If there are palettes you don't use, simply hide them in the Window menu. Also, you can drag and drop them into positions that suit you!

Crop Tool

There is a lot of power in the Crop Tool that many people don't know about, and yet it's probably one of the most used tools by photographers. Many people use the Crop Tool to remove elements of a picture, but there are a lot of hidden secrets, too, many of which we cover in this feature. Read on to find out how to correct converging verticals, expand, rotate and straighten an image, as well as ways to improve the composition

Tool preset picker: Click the arrow to show a list of preloaded Crop Tool presets.

Height and Width: Type in the dimensions that you want to constrain the crop to.

Resolution: Use to set the crop's resolution. For the best quality, type 300 pixels/inch.

Front Image and Clear: Front Image will load the image's dimensions. Clear deletes them.

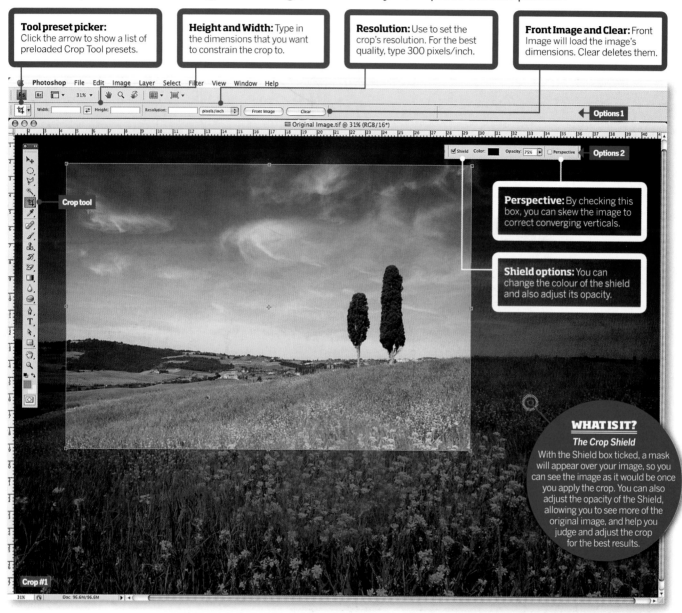

Perspective: By checking this box, you can skew the image to correct converging verticals.

Shield options: You can change the colour of the shield and also adjust its opacity.

WHAT IS IT?
The Crop Shield
With the Shield box ticked, a mask will appear over your image, so you can see the image as it would be once you apply the crop. You can also adjust the opacity of the Shield, allowing you to see more of the original image, and help you judge and adjust the crop for the best results.

CROPPING FOR COMPOSITION

Experiment with different crop shapes to strengthen your image's composition. Here, we've tried putting the focal point in the bottom third of the image, producing a square crop with the focal point in the centre of the frame and creating a panorama to show off the vista. For portraits especially, a tight crop on the subject can improve an image.

☑CROP TIP 1: EXPAND THE CANVAS

USE: GREAT FOR ADDING ARTISTIC BORDERS

When most people think of cropping, they think of removing. But it's a little-known fact that you can use the Crop Tool to add to an image. If you apply the crop constraints to an image and then pull them out, you'll be able to expand your canvas. To do this, select the **Crop Tool** and then the entire image by clicking in the top left-hand corner and dragging down to the bottom right-hand corner. If you want to add some canvas space, click on the middle widget at the top and drag it upwards. Do the same for the bottom and the sides. Use the rulers at the top and sides of the interface as a guide to make the sides even.

☑CROP TIP 2: CONSTRAIN THE CROP

USE: ACCURATE CROP TO FIT A FRAME

If you want to constrain the crop to a certain size – for instance, a 5x7in, or, in this case, 15x5in to create a panorama – you can type these dimensions in the Height and Width on the top toolbar. To do this, click on **Front Image** to load the picture's parameters in to the Height and Width panel. Type in the new dimensions – in this case, **Width**: *15in* and **Height**: *5in* – keeping the **Resolution** at *300 pixels/inch* to retain quality. Click on the image and drag the **Crop Tool** until it reaches those proportions. You can also move the position of the crop by clicking in the centre of the image and dragging it where you want it.

HOT KEY

Shift & Alt

Instead of typing in the exact proportions for Height and Width, if you hold **Alt** while using the **Crop Tool**, it will constrain the proportions for you. Also, if you would like to resize a crop before committing to it, holding **Alt** while dragging a corner widget will ensure the sides of the crop remain proportional.

HOW DO I...

Activate a crop?

There are three ways to commit to a crop: click the **tick** button in the top toolbar (to cancel a crop, click **X**); press **Enter** on your keyboard; or double-click the image itself.

☑CROP TIP 3: ROTATE THE CANVAS

USE: GOOD FOR CORRECTING WONKY HORIZONS

Unless you use a tripod with a spirit level, when you open a landscape image in Photoshop, you may find that it needs straightening. There are several ways you can do this, namely via the **Image>Image Rotation** menu, but you can also do it manually using the Crop Tool. Once you've selected the entire image with the **Crop Tool**, if you hover your cursor over the corner widgets, you'll see it change to a curved arrow. Click on the corner widget and rotate the image until the subject looks straight and commit to the crop. As the image will now be tilted, you'll find that the canvas is showing. You'll need to crop this canvas out. Alternatively, if the extra canvas space works for your image, select the **Clone Stamp Tool** and fill in the blank canvas by making a selection from the edges of the image. See page 20-21 for the Clone Stamp Tool in detail.

Secrets unlocked

☑PERSPECTIVE CORRECTION

While there are more powerful ways of correcting perspective and converging verticals, such as the Transform tools (see page 18-19), the Crop Tool is good for fixing common little problems quickly. Select the entire image with the **Crop Tool** and, as you do, you should notice the horizontal toolbar change to show Shield, Color, Opacity and Perspective. While the first three really only affect the way you see the image, Perspective is the powerful one. Often when you use a wide-angle lens to photograph a building, the image suffers from converging verticals, so the building looks like it's leaning back. Click on **Perspective** and then pull the upper-left corner widget so the line on the left matches the building's angle, then do the same thing with the right side. You'll get an image that looks like it's cropped at an angle, but then when you commit to the crop, it will straighten the image out, applying a perspective correction to it.

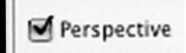

Sharpening

With so many ways to sharpen an image, it's hard to know which one will give you the best results. We tell you which to use and how...

SHARPENING IS DESIGNED to increase the clarity of an image by increasing the contrast between pixels. The aim is to sharpen each image just enough to compensate for the loss of sharpness that naturally occurs when an image is captured. Sharpening should be done with a scalpel: not a hammer. While there are myriad ways to sharpen an image – most of which can be found via the **Filter>Sharpen** menu – for ultimate control, photographers should use Smart Sharpen. The filter builds upon the excellent Unsharp Mask, providing the tools you need to get rid of certain types of blur, and work on the shadows and highlights independently. As a rule, do not sharpen in-camera, as you cannot correct it later, and while you can use the Clarity and Sharpening tools in Adobe Photoshop Raw, you are working directly with the image's pixels. If you wait to do sharpening in Photoshop, you can add a Smart Filter which, in much the same way as Adjustment Layers, creates a veneer over the image, so sharpening is non-destructive.

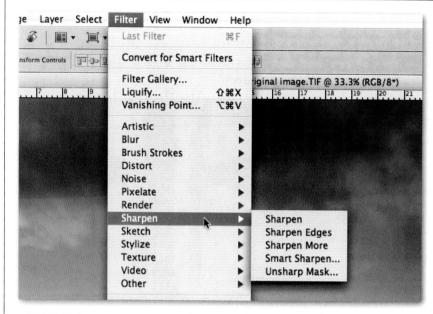

⚠ WARNING: OVERSHARPENING

When you sharpen an image too much, you'll find that areas of colour or tonal change become pixelated. You may also find that black and white marks, known as artefacts, start to show up in the image. Another indicator of oversharpening is when a halo appears around the subjects.

WHERE DO I FIND IT AND WHICH SHARPEN IS BEST FOR ME?

1) Sharpen and Sharpen More While these may seem the most obvious filters to pick from the list, they're actually the worst. The Sharpen More filter applies a stronger sharpening effect than Sharpen, but both offer no control over the way you apply them and directly affect the pixels.

2) Sharpen Edges This filter again directly affects the original pixels of an image and targets areas in the image where significant colour changes occur and sharpens them. Unlike the other filters, it only sharpens the edges of an image while preserving its overall smoothness.

3) Unsharp Mask... This is probably the most widely used way of sharpening and, until Smart Sharpen appeared, was the best method. While Smart Sharpen is considered the better option for photographers as it offers more control, you can still get great results from Unsharp Mask. It adjusts the contrast of the edge detail and creates the illusion of a sharper image. You can also add a Smart Filter to make your

adjustments non-destructive to your image. You have three sliders: Amount, which determines how much sharpening is applied; Radius, that controls how many pixels are affected; and Threshold, which determines how far different pixels must be from the surrounding area before they are considered edge pixels and sharpened. To access Unsharp Mask in Photoshop Elements 10, go to **Enhance>Unsharp Mask**.

4) Smart Sharpen... Stated to be the best way to sharpen photos by Adobe due to its precise control, Smart Sharpen builds on the features in Unsharp Mask, but with the added option of being able to sharpen the highlights and shadows separately and to remove certain types of blur. Similar settings found in Smart Sharpen can be accessed in Elements 10 by clicking **Enhance>Adjust Sharpness**, although you cannot target shadows and highlights independently, but you can target areas in need of sharpening by clicking **More Refined**.

🔧 Tooled up!

☑ SHARPEN TOOL

Historically, the Sharpen Tool is the easiest but worst method of sharpening an image, as it introduces a host of artefacts. Now, with CS5, it has new algorithms that have made it the most powerful way to sharpen, as you can sharpen selectively and precisely using its brush. It's also tuned so it does not create artefacts.

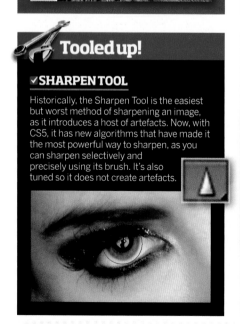

🔒 Secrets unlocked

☑ THE 'SMART' WAY TO FILTER

Whenever you use a filter, it's a good idea to convert your image to a Smart Filter first by clicking **Filter>Convert for Smart Filters**. Like an Adjustment Layer, a Smart Filter allows you to make alterations without affecting the original pixels of the image and allows you to revert back to editing the filter later, no matter how far you've gone into the editing process. Once you convert your image layer to a Smart Filter, you can pick your chosen filter – in this case, **Filter>Sharpen** – and make your adjustments. When you click **OK** and the dialogue box closes, you'll find your Layers palette has an extra layer called Smart Filters and below that the name of the filter you've applied (eg Unsharp Mask). If you ever need to make further adjustments, double-click on the part labelled **Unsharp Mask**. You can also adjust the **Opacity** of the filter by clicking on the symbol to its right.

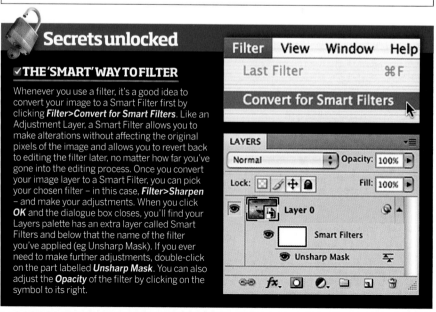

Sharpening your images

Unsharp Mask is an age-old favourite for most photographers and can give great results, but for ultimate control and ability to reduce destructive artefacts, it's time to smarten up about the way you sharpen

1 UNSHARP MASK...
GOOD SHARPEN FOR ALL LEVELS

For the majority of photographers, this filter offers adequate control over sharpening. Before you make any adjustments, enlarge the **Preview** image to **100%** to see the effects of the sharpening. While each image is different, for a high-resolution image it's best to adjust the **Amount** between **150-200%**, set the **Radius** to **1-2** pixels and the **Threshold** between **2-20**. When sharpening for the web, increase the **Amount** to around **400%**, reduce the **Radius** to less than **1** pixel and the **Threshold** to **0**, as there's less information.

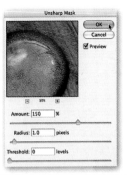
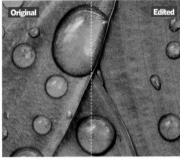

HOT TIP

Preview the original
If you want to see the image before sharpening was applied, hover over the preview image until the hand cursor appears and then hold it down to temporarily revert the image back to its original state.

2 SMART SHARPEN...
ONCE MASTERED, THE BEST SHARPEN

The Smart Sharpen dialogue box has several controls, including tabs Basic and Advanced. So you can focus on the basic adjustments first, click on the **Advanced** tab and set all the sliders to **0**. Back at the **Sharpen** tab, at the bottom of the dialogue box is a drop-down menu called **Remove**, which offers three ways of sharpening an image: Gaussian Blur, Lens Blur and Motion Blur. Unsharp Mask works to remove Gaussian Blur, but there's actually very little Gaussian Blur in an image and much more Lens Blur which, if reduced, targets halos and the finer details. Motion Blur is brilliant for reducing ghosting and slight camera shake. Unfortunately, it's not very intuitive, so you need to specify the angle of the motion. You can either do this by trial and error, moving the angle dial around until you can see the blur reduce in the preview, or use the **Ruler Tool** in the toolbar to measure the direction of the motion blur and then input the degree in the **Smart Sharpen Angle** box. Make sure the box called **More Accurate** is checked, too, before you adjust the settings, as this will ensure only the areas that need sharpening have it applied. The sliders work in the same way as Unsharp Mask in that there's an **Amount** (set between **50%** and **150%**) and **Radius** (**1-2** pixels). Now, to target any artefacts or halos caused by the sharpening, click on the **Advanced** tab and either **Shadows** or **Highlights** (depending on where the artefacts are). You can then use the **Fade Amount** slider to selectively reduce the sharpening in that area and the **Tonal Width** to control the tonal range modified and the radius. You may need to enlarge the preview to 200% to really judge the effects.

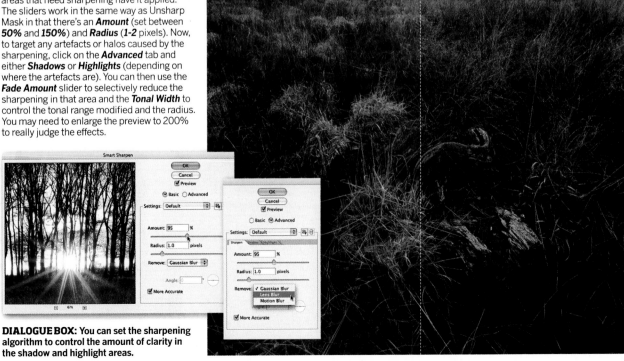

DIALOGUE BOX: You can set the sharpening algorithm to control the amount of clarity in the shadow and highlight areas.

Noise

Noise can be the bane of digital photographers. We tell you how to minimise noise to improve quality

NOISE IS AN unsightly and so far unavoidable side effect of digital capture. This form of electronic interference is usually revealed by underexposure, high ISOs and shooting in dark environments with a long shutter speed. Much of an image's noise is embedded in the shadows, which is why, if you're shooting in Raw, it's always better to slightly overexpose a scene than underexpose it, as long as you're careful not to blow the highlights. When an image is darkened, the tonal range is compressed, hiding the noise, but if you try to lighten a digital image in Photoshop, you'll find coloured and light specks emerge from the shadows as the tonal range is expanded, making it look grainy.

There are two types of noise: chromatic that appears as red, green and blue specks; and luminance, which is when an image looks like it's been sprinkled with salt and pepper. Reducing either type of noise improves image quality, but can also soften the image, so you need to find a good balance between noise control and retaining edge detail.

Photoshop CS4 and Elements 9 handle noise reduction in the same way and do a fairly good job of it. There are plug-ins and software that are dedicated to noise reduction, too, such as Noise Ninja and Nik Software's Dfine 2.0, which may handle high levels of noise better. Since CS5, Adobe Camera Raw offers a lot more control over noise reduction, which is ideal because you'll be working on an image when it has the maximum information. For CS4 and Elements, though, we'd advise using Photoshop filters as you can apply a Smart Filter first, allowing you to edit changes later and leave the original image pixels untouched.

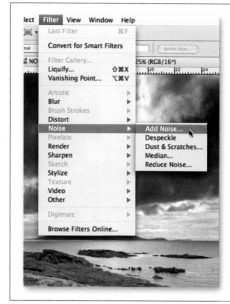

FINDING THE NOISE FILTER

1) Add Noise... This applies randomly coloured or monochromatic pixels to an image and is mainly used for creative effect.

2) Despeckle Directly affecting the image's pixels, Despeckle targets luminance noise but is the only noise filter not to offer photographers control over how it's applied.

3) Dust and Scratches... Enables you to hide picture faults such as hair, scratches and dust using two sliders: Radius and Threshold. The Radius determines the size of the area that's searched for dissimilar pixels. The Threshold value determines how dissimilar the pixels should be before they're eliminated.

4) Median... Although it only has one control (Radius), Median is widely used and does a good job of smoothing out noise while automatically preserving edge detail.

5) Reduce Noise... For the most control over how you reduce noise, retain detail and to target the different colour channels independently, the Reduce Noise filter is the one to use.

☑ NOISE TIP: IMAGE STACKS

USE: TO COMPRISE A NOISE-FREE IMAGE

As noise appears differently in every frame, if you shoot a series of images from the same viewpoint and stack them in Photoshop CS4 or CS5 (Extended), it can automatically create an image with minimal noise by selecting areas that hold the least amount of noise. Click *File>Scripts>Load Images into Stack* and select your images by clicking *Browse*. Tick *Attempt to Automatically Align and Create Smart Object*, and then *OK*. Once it's finished processing, go to *Layer>Smart Object>Stack Mode* where a menu of options appear, each a command that determines how each layer interacts. Select *Median* as this targets the transparent pixels and smooths out any noise in the shadows. It also removes any unwanted elements, such as moving subjects that aren't present in every image.

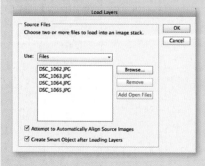

☑ NOISE TIP: DUST AND SCRATCHES...

USE: REMOVE SMALL MARKS FROM AN IMAGE

To get rid of noise and small imperfections, like the ones you get from scanning in an old photo, select *Filter>Noise>Dust & Scratches*. Set a *Radius* between *1* and *4* to eliminate defects (any bigger and the image will blur), and adjust the *Threshold* between *0* and *128* to bring back detail.

Original

HOT TIP

Smart Filter

Before you apply a filter, convert your image to a Smart Filter as it allows you to make alterations without affecting the image's original pixels, as well as correct adjustments to the image later. To do this, with the image layer selected, click *Filter>Convert for Smart Filter* then select the filter you wish to apply from the menu (Noise, Sharpen, Texture etc), all of which have their own sub-menus.

Secrets unlocked

☑ NOISE AND ADOBE CAMERA RAW

When you open your image in Adobe Camera Raw, under the Detail tab you'll find noise reduction options have been expanded to include more controls in addition to CS4's Luminance and Color, allowing for similar control as you would get with the Reduce Noise filter in Photoshop. Zoom in to an area of shadow at least *200%* and set all the sliders to *0*. Drag the *Color* slider to the right until all the red, blue and green specks disappear. Next, move the *Luminance* slider until the white specks are reduced, being careful to watch for loss in detail. Then use a combination of *Luminance Detail*, *Luminance Contrast* and *Color Detail* to bring back some of the edge details you may have lost.

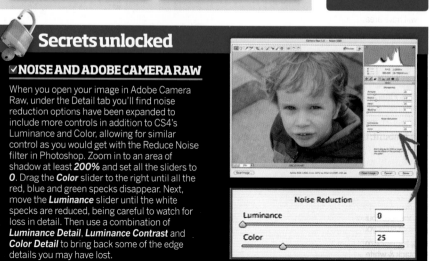

How to reduce (or add) noise in your pictures

Noise has the power to make or break a picture. Find out the best way to reduce chromatic & luminance noise in Photoshop as well as how it can be used creatively to give an image a gritty, old-time edge

1 REDUCE NOISE FILTER
IMPROVE IMAGES SHOT AT A HIGH ISO

This is one of the most effective ways of reducing noise as it offers a lot of control, enabling photographers to preserve detail as well as target noise. In its basic form, you have four controls: Strength, Preserve Details, Reduce Color Noise and Sharpen Details.

■**Strength:** This controls the impact of the filter and you'll notice the higher you set it, the more an image is softened and detail is reduced.

■**Preserve Details:** Using this control, you can specify the level of detail that should be kept so an image is not rendered blurry when noise reduction is applied.

■**Reduce Color Noise:** Controls how much chromatic noise is reduced.

■**Sharpen Detail:** Restores sharpness in places noise reduction softens.

For the best results, take all the sliders back to **0** and zoom in to the image preview to at least **200%**; you want to see the filter's effect on the pixels. Adjust the **Strength** setting first, checking the image's shadows, highlights and mid-tone areas for noise. If your image has a lot of colour noise, you should adjust the **Reduce Color Noise** slider in conjunction with the **Strength** slider until you're happy with the noise level. Now slowly drag the **Preserve Detail** slider to the right until you start to see the noise reappear in the image. Set a value of **100** to preserve the most image detail but reduce luminance noise the least.

When using the **Reduce Noise** filter, click on the **Remove JPEG Artifact** option. One of the side effects of compressing your image to JPEG format is it will create box-like patterns of pixels. Using this setting, Photoshop smooths over the artifacts, making them less pronounced.

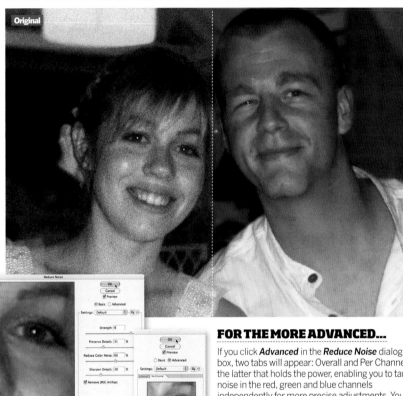

DIALOGUE BOX: Click the *Advanced* button to access options for more targeted noise reduction in the separate colour channels.

FOR THE MORE ADVANCED...

If you click **Advanced** in the **Reduce Noise** dialogue box, two tabs will appear: Overall and Per Channel. It's the latter that holds the power, enabling you to target noise in the red, green and blue channels independently for more precise adjustments. You may find that luminance noise is more prominent in the Blue channel. Once you pick your Channel from the drop-down menu, you need to adjust the two sliders: **Strength** and **Preserve Detail**. For the best results, balance both these sliders. **Strength** determines the amount of noise reduction applied while **Preserve Detail** mellows the effect by maintaining edge details.

2 ADD NOISE FILTER
GIVE YOUR IMAGES AN OLD FILM EFFECT

Most of the time, photographers want to minimise noise, but there are occasions when it can be used for creative effect, such as if you want to make a black & white picture look older than it is. It's also useful to blend areas that have been retouched. For instance, if you paint over an area or apply blur, chances are you will have areas that look smooth amongst areas of noise. Adding a bit of noise to the retouched area can help it look less obvious. When adding noise, it's a good idea to work on a duplicate image layer so you're not affecting the image's original pixels and can undo any adjustments you make. With your image open, go to **Layer> Duplicate Layer** and then click **Filter>Noise>Add Noise** and adjust the filter's settings as you see fit, before clicking **OK**.

These are the three main settings:

■ **Amount:** Use this slider to control how much noise is applied.

■ **Distribution:** This determines how the noise is applied. Uniform keeps noise consistent throughout the image, while Gaussian produces a more speckled effect that in some cases makes the noise more pronounced. Experiment to see what suits your image.

■**Monochromatic:** Makes the noise black & white.

HOT KEY

Alt to reset

If you hold down **Alt**, the Cancel button in the dialogue box will change to Reset so you can revert back to the original image and start again. This will work for most of the dialogue boxes you use.

HOT TIP

Preview the original

If you want to see the image before noise was applied, hover over the preview image until a hand cursor appears and then hold it down to temporarily change the image back.

Transform

NO KEYBOARD SHORTCUTS

Learn how to scale, skew, rotate and generally 'transform' your image to get a better result

EACH OF THE TRANSFORM commands enable you to change a different geometric aspect of a layer or pixel selection. They are powerful but destructive tools, working by manipulating pixels, but can also be very useful if you need to correct lens distortion or if you have to change the shape and size of a subject. Among the commands that allow you to manually adjust layers are preset commands for common rotations and flip orientations.

Transform only affects layers selected in the Layers palette (**Window>Layers**). If you want to adjust all your image's layers simultaneously, click on the top layer, then the bottom layer while holding down **Shift**. Or hold **Cmd** and select the layers you want to alter individually. For you to transform any image in Photoshop CS4, you will first need to unlock the Background layer in your Layers palette by double-clicking on it, giving it a name when the dialogue box appears, then clicking **OK**. In Photoshop Elements 9, however, it automatically unlocks the Background layer once you try to use the Transform commands.

To access the commands in Photoshop CS4, click **Edit>Transform** for the drop-down menu to appear. Once you've selected your tool, a bounding box appears around the image. If you're using Elements 9, you can access the commands via **Image>Transform**. Both packages offer Free Transform, which we'll cover later, and is the most powerful command comprising all of the Transform commands (except Warp), but it's also the trickiest to use. To get started, you may find it easier to use one of the specialised commands detailed here so that you do not have to worry about inadvertently adjusting the picture in the wrong direction.

WHERE DO I FIND THE COMMANDS AND WHAT DO THEY DO?

1) Again (**Ctrl+Shift+T**) Once you've applied a transform command, click **Again** to repeat the command. It's useful if you need to make the same precise adjustments to several images.

2) Scale Resize the image by clicking on the corner anchor points of the bounding box, holding **Shift** to constrain the proportions.

3) Rotate This enables you to manually turn an image or selection, as opposed to using the preset 90° increments found later down the Transform menu. Place the cursor outside the bounding box and rotate the image left or right once the bent arrow appears. You can hold down **Shift** to constrain the rotation to 15° increments.

4) Skew This can be used to correct or apply slants in an image. For instance, if an image has a building that looks like it's leaning, you can use this command to straighten it.

5) Distort Use the command to stretch the image in any direction you pull it in. Hold down the **Ctrl** key while adjusting the bounding box to distort the layer or hold down **Alt** if you want to make the distortion symmetrical.

6) Perspective You can either make objects look like they're further away from you or closer to you by stretching or compressing the image. Drag the corner anchor points to adjust the perspective of the image to correct distortion or creative effect.

7) Warp Manipulate up to nine sectors of an image by pushing and pulling the pixels in any direction using the Warp command. It will curve and bend the edges of an image or selection. Photoshop Elements 9 doesn't have this command, but you can use the Liquify Filter for similar effects.

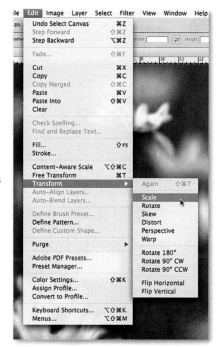

8) Rotate & Flip The bottom two sections of the menu hold some common preset commands for quick adjustments. They include rotating layers in 90° increments and flipping them vertically or horizontally. Simple stuff!

☑ TRANSFORM TIP 1: WARP

USE: CHANGE A SUBJECT'S SHAPE

The Warp transform is suited to changing the shape of large parts of a picture, compared to the Liquify Filter that is better for applying intricate distortions. Warp is infamously used to make subjects look slimmer in portraits.

You can access it via **Edit>Transform** or, if you're already using the Transform tools, by clicking the **Switch Between Free Transform** and **Warp Mode** button in the top toolbar. By using this button, it means you can make Free Transform adjustments and Warp adjustments in one transformation, reducing the degradation of the image.

The toolbar also offers a selection of preset warp options for you to use. When in Warp mode, you can control the shape of the image by moving the Bezier handles at each corner of the bounding box, which comprises nine sections that you can adjust.

☑ TRANSFORM TIP 2: PERSPECTIVE

USE: CORRECT LENS DISTORTION CAUSED BY CAMERA TILT

When using a wide-angle lens for landscapes, at its widest focal length you may find your image suffers from either barrel distortion (when the image looks like it's been mapped around a sphere, ie curves extend outwards) or keystoning (when the subject looks narrower at the top than the bottom). To correct this type of distortion, open your image and activate the rulers (**View>Rulers**). Pull a guide from the ruler to match up with a subject in the image that should be straight, such as a wall or a tree. Now click **Edit>Transform>Perspective** to activate the bounding box and drag the corner anchor points inwards or outwards to adjust the image's perspective. Use the guide as a marker to tell when the distorted image has been straightened correctly.

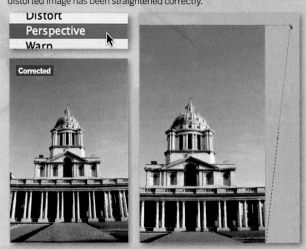

HOT TIP

Adjust the Opacity
When transforming a selection, and trying to align it with the layer beneath, try adjusting the layer's opacity using the **Opacity** slider at the top of the Layers palette. It will make the layer semi-transparent so you can see the image beneath it.

HOT KEY

Ctrl+0
Often if you're transforming an image, the bounding box will become larger than the canvas making it difficult to get to the anchor points. If you press **Cmd+0** (**Ctrl+0** for PC), you will quickly zoom out of your image far enough to reveal the transform bounding box.

Free Transform

PC QUICK SELECT KEYS = | T

MAC QUICK SELECT KEYS =

Take complete control over reshaping your image using the Free Transform command

FREE TRANSFORM is the most versatile command, but also the toughest to use, allowing you to scale, distort, rotate, skew and adjust perspective using a combination of modifier key combinations (see below) in conjunction with moving different anchor points. You can access this via *Edit>Free Transform* or clicking on the *Move Tool* and checking the *Show Transform Controls* box in the top toolbar.

You can also apply transforms to individual selections, using the Transform Selection command. This tool works exactly the same way as Free Transform and you are able to use the same modifier key combinations listed below. Make your selection using a selection tool such as the Magnetic Lasso, and click *Select>Transform Selection*. Before you are able to make any transform adjustments, you'll need to commit to the selection by pressing *Enter*. You then have a number of options:

■ **Change the height and width:** Click an anchor point on any side of the bounding box and drag to adjust the height or width separately.

■ **Scale:** Click a corner anchor point to adjust the height and width simultaneously and hold down the *Shift* key if at the same if you want to lock the proportions to avoid distorting the image. Alternatively, hold down the *Alt* key while dragging a corner anchor point to scale the selection around the crosshair in the centre of the bounding box, which you can move anywhere in the selection to change the point of transformation. Hold down *Shift* and *Alt* to constrain the proportions of the scale.

■ **Rotate:** Click outside the bounding box by one of the anchor points and a curved arrow will appear, click and rotate left or right.

■ **Skew:** Hold down the *Cmd* (Mac) or *Ctrl* (PC) key and drag a side anchor point in, out, up and down.

■ **Distort:** Hold down the *Cmd* (Mac) or *Ctrl* (PC) key and drag a corner anchor point in any direction.

■ **Perspective:** Hold down the *Cmd* (Mac) or *Ctrl* (PC) key and drag the bounding box's four corner anchor points inwards or out to adjust perspective.

1 To use Free Transform, select from the *Edit* menu or use *Ctrl + T* with the image selected.

2 Hold outside one of the anchor points and move cursor to rotate.

3 Hold the *Cmd* key and drag a anchor point to distort the image.

4 Drag any corner or side tab to adjust image height and width.

Secrets unlocked

✓ USING SMART OBJECTS

By converting your layers into a Smart Object before you use the Transform commands, any transformation is applied to the Smart Object and not the original pixels. It also means you can go back and edit the adjustment after you've committed to it. Do this by selecting the layers in the Layers palette that you want to transform, then click on the layers panel options and choose *Convert to Smart Object*.

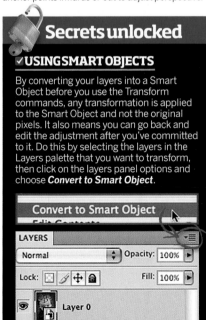

✓ FREE TRANSFORM TIP: CTRL + CLICK

USE: MULTIPLE COMMANDS TO PRESERVE QUALITY

As the Transform commands directly affect the pixels of your image, every time you apply a transformation, you degrade the image quality. You can minimise the destruction by applying all your transformations before committing to the adjustments – for instance, change the perspective, scale and rotation before pressing *Enter*. When in Free Transform, you can switch to the more constrained transform commands such as Skew and Scale by holding *Ctrl* and clicking on the image.

HOT KEY

ctrl Z

Undo last command

You can undo your last adjustment using a transform command by clicking *Ctrl+Z* (PC) or *Cmd+Z* (Mac). You can also use it to revert back to the original image once the transform command has been applied. Any loss of quality caused by a transform command will also be restored.

Clone Stamp Tool

Find out the hidden secrets of the Clone Stamp Tool that will make replacing pixels that much easier

THE CLONE STAMP TOOL is one of the most powerful retouching tools in Photoshop's arsenal. And while it can get rid of distracting elements in a photograph, it can also add parts to an image to make it more interesting. The Clone Stamp Tool works by sampling pixels from a source layer and applying them to a target layer (the target layer can be the same layer or a different layer). To make a source

sample, click *Alt* and click on the area you want to replace. It's a powerful tool that, rather than masking the area like other retouching tools, copies and replaces pixels. Before you start any retouching, create a new layer (*Layer>New*) and select *Sample: All Layers* in the top toolbar. By cloning to a new layer, you protect the original image pixels so you can reverse any changes you make.

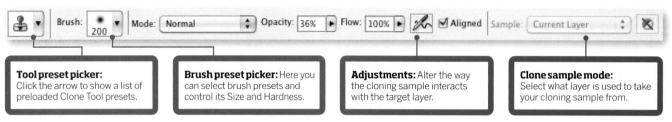

Tool preset picker:
Click the arrow to show a list of preloaded Clone Tool presets.

Brush preset picker: Here you can select brush presets and control its Size and Hardness.

Adjustments: Alter the way the cloning sample interacts with the target layer.

Clone sample mode:
Select what layer is used to take your cloning sample from.

1 Create a new layer (*Layer>New*) and select the *Clone Stamp Tool* and *All Layers* from the Sample menu in the Options toolbar. Zoom into the area to clone out and set the *Opacity* to *100%*.

2 Take a source sample of pixels from near the target area by holding *Alt* and brush over the target area using small stroking motions to avoid leaving signs of clicking the mouse.

3 The edges of cloning can look quite harsh, so reduce the brush's *Hardness* to *20%*, leaving the *Opacity* at *100%*. Also try adjusting the *Flow* for more subtle control over the cloning.

4 Cloning in a different area can create a repeat pattern if the sample is too close to the target. If this happens, undo your changes and then clone from an area further away from the target but on the same plane of focus.

HOT KEY
Brackets
Brushes are accessed via the top toolbar or via *Window>Brushes*. While you're working on an image, if you need to alter the size of your brush, press the right or the left square brackets (next to the letter P).

Secrets unlocked

☑ WORKFLOW ASSISTANCE

1) Create a 'shadow' window
Click *Window>Arrange>New Window for [filename]* to create a shadow image. Now you can zoom into the working image and have the shadow image open to see the overall effect, saving you from zooming in and out.

2) Create a preview overlay
Activate the *Show Overlay* and the *Clipped* checkbox in the Clone Source panel (*Window> Clone Source* or *Shift+Alt*) to see an overlay of the image as you clone it.

☑ CLONE TIP:
CLONE FROM ANOTHER IMAGE

USE: ADD ELEMENTS TO AN IMAGE

Open the source image and the target image in Photoshop and then align the documents side by side, by dragging one off the other. Now select the *Clone Stamp Tool* and tick the *Aligned* box in the top toolbar. Select a soft brush and take a selection from the sample picture, in this case the clouds, and then paint the source where you want it on the target image. You may find adjusting the *Opacity* helps improve the results.

Healing Brush Tool

PC & MAC QUICK SELECT KEY
FOR PHOTOSHOP CS & ELEMENTS =

Learn how to use the Healing Brush Tool and its various sub-tools to improve your retouching techniques

IMAGES OFTEN HAVE unwanted marks – such as imperfections like spots or wrinkles on portraits – that all need minimising. The Healing Brush Tool is the main device for doing this kind of retouching, but there are several sub-tools such as the Patch Tool and Spot Healing Brush Tool that do the same thing: hiding unwanted elements, but working in different ways and having different effects. The Healing Brush Tool works by matching the texture, luminosity and colour of the sample with the target area, so it blends with the pixels around it. As the Healing Brush spreads, it's useful to use a hard-edged brush. The tool also struggles on edges or areas of high contrast as it does not know how to blend tones, and it doesn't have the Opacity setting found on the Clone Stamp Tool.

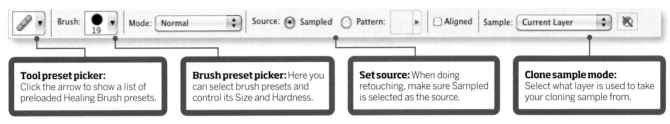

Tool preset picker: Click the arrow to show a list of preloaded Healing Brush presets.

Brush preset picker: Here you can select brush presets and control its Size and Hardness.

Set source: When doing retouching, make sure Sampled is selected as the source.

Clone sample mode: Select what layer is used to take your cloning sample from.

1 Create a new layer (*Layer>New*), select the *Healing Brush Tool* and a hard-edged brush, and click *All Layers* from the *Sample* menu in the top toolbar. Zoom into the areas you want to clean up.

2 Take a sample from close to the area that you want to clear up by clicking *Alt/Option*. Brush over the areas with the blemishes and alter the *Size* and *Hardness* of the brush as you go along.

3 As the Healing Brush Tool brushes over an area of contrast, it can smudge as it struggles to match the varying tonality. It's best to take samples close to the target area.

4 Be careful not to overdo the Healing Brush Tool's effect: you don't want to eliminate all imperfections as your subject will look like a porcelain doll. To avoid this, vary the opacity by clicking *Edit>Fade Healing Brush*.

HOT TIP

Aligned
When this option is ticked in the top toolbar, the sample points are aligned with the tool as it moves. This means every time you release the mouse you need to take a new sample. When *Aligned* is deselected, the original selection is locked in and used for every new stroke.

Secrets unlocked

✓ CS5'S CONTENT AWARE FILL

If you want easy, clean removal of unwanted photo elements, then you need to try CS5's Content-Aware Fill option, which automatically removes objects by filling the area with the pixels around it, matching the lighting, tone and noise of the surrounding area. It can be achieved by either using the *Spot Healing Brush Tool* and ticking the *Content-Aware Fill* option in the top toolbar, or by making a selection using a tool such as the Lasso Tool, then clicking *Edit>Fill>Content Aware Fill*.

SUB TOOL: SPOT HEALING BRUSH

USE: CLEAN UP DUST SPECKS

This tool works best on areas of low detail as it lacks the user control of the other retouching tools. Instead of being able to take a sample, you click on the area you want to hide and this tool will automatically take a sample of the pixels around it to match the target area. It's ideal for cleaning up dust specks.

SUB TOOL: PATCH TOOL

USE: BE MORE SELECTIVE

One of the more intelligent tools, the Patch Tool uses a selection instead of a brush. There are two ways you can apply this tool: draw a selection of a good area and drag it on top of a damaged area and select *Destination* in the top toolbar; or select a bad area and drag it on to a good area and select *Source* in the toolbar.

SUB TOOL: RED-EYE TOOL

USE: CORRECT RED-EYE

When a subject looks directly into a camera's on-camera flash it often causes them to get red-eye (where the pupils are rendered red). To correct this and return the subject's eye colour back to normal, select the *Red-Eye Tool*, zoom in to the subject's eye and click on the red pupil once to see the colour disappear.

Layers & Layer Masks

Working with Layers is not essential for basic image editing, but for those photographers who want to take their images to the next level, they are a fundamental part of your editing workflow

LAYERS ARE THE BUILDING blocks of non-destructive image editing, giving you the opportunity to construct an image in stages and the flexibility to make any edits at any time. With this in mind, hopefully by the end of this feature you'll have a better understanding of how to get the most from Layers so your editing can become more selective and sophisticated whether using Elements or CS.

When you open an image in Photoshop, your image automatically becomes the Background layer in the Layers palette (accessible via **Windows>Layers**), which is located via the **Tools** menu. You cannot edit the Background layer as it's locked, but you can make it editable by double-clicking on the padlock symbol. Most of the time it's advisable to keep this Background layer locked and, instead, create a duplicate layer (**Layer>Duplicate Layer**) to work on. By doing this, it means at least one layer of your image still retains the unedited, original pixels, so if you make a mistake and want to start again, all you need to do is delete the extra layers and you're back where you started.

It's best to think of layers as clear sheets of acetate stacked on top of each other, each featuring a part of your image (object or effect) that, when merged together, create your final picture. The three types of layers we'll be covering here are transparent layers (layers without any pixels) that you can add pixels to, image layers that contain duplicate pixels from the original image or parts of a different photo, and Adjustment Layers, which we'll cover in depth later on. Layers allow you to combine parts of different photos, but for basic photography editing, this usually doesn't stretch further than replacing a sky in a dull landscape, adding a few extra people to a street scene or switching frowning faces in a group shot for smiles. However, there are some photographers and digital artists that take it to a higher level, using multiple layers and objects from different images to literally construct their picture from scratch. We'll only cover the basics here, but the internet and Adobe's website is bursting with more advanced techniques if you wish to delve in to this realm called compositing.

THE LAYERS PALETTE

1) Blend Mode This accesses the drop-down menu of layer blending modes that control how the layers interact with one another.

2) Opacity Use this slider to adjust the transparency of the layer, controlling how much of the layer beneath it shows through.

3) Lock transparent pixels/image pixels These two buttons enable you to lock an individual layer so only image or transparent pixels can be edited, respectively.

4) Lock position Use this to prevent your image from moving rank in the Layers palette. Click once to lock and again to unlock.

5) Lock all Apply this lock to any layer that you want to protect from editing. If you want to unlock a layer, highlight it and press the lock button again.

6) Layer visibility Click the eye icon to make the adjacent layer invisible. Click it again to make the layer visible.

7) Link Use this option to link multiple layers together.

8) Select layers You can tell which layer you've got selected by whether it's highlighted blue. Select multiple layers by holding down **Cmd** and clicking on each to select them.

9) Background Layer This is your original image. Keep it locked so it cannot be edited.

10) Add Layer Style Access a variety of styles from Blend Modes to drop shadows and outer glows. They're special effects that work well with objects and text.

11) New Adjustment Layer Click here to access a list of all the Adjustment Layers.

12) Create New Group Use this to group layers together into a folder to contain your editing to a few selected layers.

13) Create New Layer Click to apply an empty, transparent layer. Or click and drag an image layer down on to the icon to duplicate it.

14) Trash Can Highlight the layer, or Layer Mask, and click the bin to delete it or, alternatively, click and drag them on to the Trash Can.

HOW TO CREATE A NEW LAYER

If you want a transparent layer, either click the **Create New Layer** icon at the bottom of the Layers palette or go to **Layer>New>Layer**. If you want a layer with the same pixels as your original image, you can duplicate the Background layer by dragging it down to the **Create New Layer** button or by clicking **Layer> Duplicate Layer**. To copy parts of one image on to another, you first need to make your selection from the source image and then press **Ctrl/ Cmd+C** to copy it. Revert back to your destination image and press **Ctrl/Cmd+V** to paste it on the image. Or using the **Move Tool**, click and drag the selection from the source image to the destination image (press **Ctrl/ Cmd+A** to move the whole picture). The new image will immediately create a new layer above the destination image. Then use the **Move Tool** to reposition your selection.

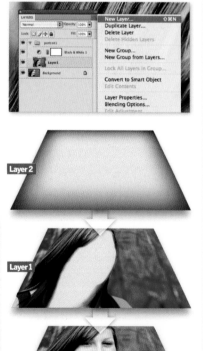

HOW LAYER ORDER WORKS

Every new layer that's created automatically sits on top of the layer before it in the Layers palette and its effect or pixels will affect every layer that's underneath it. Use the **Move Tool** to re-order the layers.

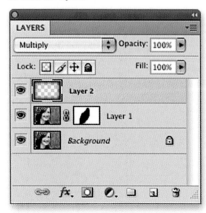

Workflow tools

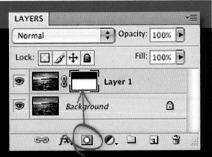

✓ LAYER MASKS

Layer Masks are extremely powerful editing tools as they enable you to localise your edits to specific parts of an image. You can apply them to any layer – Adjustment Layers have one already attached (see next page for more details) – and use the Brush Tool to 'paint' areas in or out of the layer that you want to make visible in your final image. Layer Masks are a new feature to Elements 9 and are accessible in the same way as CS via the **Add Layer Mask** icon at the bottom of the Layers palette or **Layer>Layer Mask>Reveal All** or **Hide All**. When added, a Layer Mask appears next to the layer it's linked to in the Layers palette. As its default, or when set to **Reveal All**, a Layer Mask appears white and doesn't affect any pixel until you paint on it. When set to **Hide All**, a Layer Mask is filled with black and will hide all the pixels in the image layer until you

use white paint on the mask to reveal the pixels. It's a forgiving process for editing your layers, although it does take practice and requires you to adjust the Size and Hardness of your brush to get a smooth, accurate finish. Another way is to select and refine the area you want to keep visible, then apply the Layer Mask. You can do this by clicking **Layer>Layer Mask>Reveal Selection** or **Hide Selection**, if it's the area you want invisible.

Secrets unlocked

✓ LAYER MASK HOT KEYS

SHIFT To temporarily disable a mask, hold **Shift** and click on the **Layer Mask thumbnail** so a red cross appears through it. Click the thumbnail again to restore it.

ALT The Layer Mask thumbnail gives a small indication of what you're painting on the mask. To see an image-sized version, hold down **Alt** and click on the thumbnail.

COMMAND Once you've painted the areas you want to adjust on the layer mask, hold **Cmd** and click on the mask to convert the area into a selection.

Editing images using Layers and Layer Masks

Learn to improve your photos post-capture by replacing unwanted parts with something more appealing

1 Here, we have a landscape image with a dull sky but an impressive foreground. By exchanging the sky for one with more interest, it should dramatically improve the image. Open both images in Photoshop and, using the **Move Tool**, drag the landscape image on top of the sky picture.

2 The sky image now features two layers in its Layers palette, with the landscape picture on top. With that layer selected, apply a Layer Mask by clicking on the **Add Layer Mask** icon at the bottom of the Layers palette. Reduce the **Opacity** of the top layer so the sky image shows through.

3 Move the image so the new sky covers the old one entirely. Now select the **Brush Tool** and reduce the **Hardness** to below **10%** to give it a soft edge, and select **Black** as your **Foreground color**. With the **Layer Mask** selected, paint on the image to hide the old sky and reveal the new one.

4 Once you've finished and roughly gone around the objects on the horizon, increase the layer's **Opacity** back to **100%**. Now zoom in to the horizon and, using a smaller brush, go around the areas of the landscape you might have missed. Use **White** paint to restore any foreground.

HOW DO I...

Delete a Layer Mask?
Click on the link (looks like a paperclip icon) in between the image and Layer Mask thumbnail. This will unlink the two so you can click and drag the Layer Mask in to the trash at the bottom of the Layers palette. Or hold **Ctrl** and click the **Layer Mask** to access a menu with **Delete Layer Mask**.

HOT KEY

To decrease or increase the size of your brush, click [or] respectively. To toggle between Black and White paint, to hide or reveal detail, simply press **X**.

HOT TIP

By default, the Layer Mask button in the Layers palette creates a Reveal All mask. If you want to add a Hide All Layer Mask, hold down **Alt** while clicking the same button.

Adjustment Layers

For non-destructive editing, you can't beat Adjustment Layers for ease of use and flexibility. Here, we explain the basics to using these invaluable layers so you can be more selective with your editing

BEFORE ADJUSTMENT LAYERS were introduced, photographers would have to duplicate the Background layer to avoid editing or damaging the original image. While you can still do this, Adjustment Layers allow you to apply adjustments like Curves, Levels or Hue/Saturation as a separate layer that you can refine, change or delete at any time during your editing process.

The alternative would be to apply an adjustment command via *Image>Adjustments* directly to a duplicated image layer, but this won't give you the flexibility of editing the effect after you've committed to it. Plus, if you want to get rid of the adjustment's effect, you'll have to delete the whole image layer, which can be frustrating if you've applied different adjustments to the image layer you need to delete. Most of the usual adjustment commands are available as an Adjustment Layer, making it a much more favourable way to edit pictures, but it's still worth checking out the Adjustments menu for those commands you can't access as a separate layer.

Being able to control how an adjustment affects your image post-application means you're not committed to any adjustment command you use, making the process a lot more forgiving and fluid. Not only can you reverse or delete an adjustment, you can temporarily hide them the same way you would an image layer, you can apply a blending mode or fine-tune the effect by changing the Opacity and you can restrict the effect using Layer Masks.

An Adjustment Layer can be created in one of three ways: by clicking *Layer>New Adjustment Layer* and selecting your required adjustment; clicking on the Adjustment icon (half black/half white circle) at the bottom of the Layers palette to access the same list of options; or by opening the Adjustments panel via the Windows menu. Any of those work, but some are quicker than others and offer you more options: you just need to find the one you work with the most efficiently.

ADJUSTMENT LAYERS PANEL

By opening the Adjustments panel, you get immediate access to all adjustment presets and the 15 core Adjustment Layers at the click of a button. When you select an Adjustment Layer from the panel, the Adjustments panel converts into a control panel for the command with the tools to refine the effect. Click back on to the Layers palette to close and convert the control panel back to the Adjustments panel. Have a go to see what we mean…

1) Add an adjustment: Click on the half white/half black icon at the bottom of the Layers palette to access Adjustment Layers. Click on the adjustment you want to apply.

2) Presets: Click the drop-down menus of each of the Adjustment Layers to access their loaded presets, normally located at the top of the specific Adjustment Layer's control panel.

3) Expand View: Click here to enlarge the Adjustment panel. It can be useful if you're working with Curves or Levels and need a larger area to view the adjustment graphs.

4) Clip the Adjustment Layer: Click here to clip an Adjustment Layer to the layer directly below it in the Layers palette so it's the only one that's affected by the adjustment.

5) Layer visibility: Click on the eye to temporarily switch off the Adjustment Layer. It's useful to toggle between visible and invisible to see the effect of the Adjustment Layer on the original image.

6) Review: If you re-edit an Adjustment Layer, click and hold this button to revert back to the Adjustment Layer's original state to see whether your re-editing has improved or worsened the overall effect of your image.

7) Reset: Click here to reset the Adjustment Layer back to its default settings.

8) Delete: Click the trash can to delete the current Adjustment Layer.

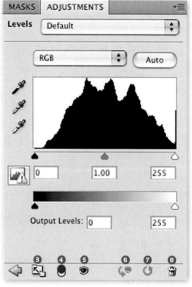

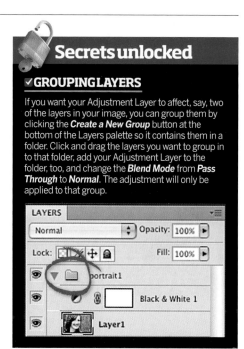

Secrets unlocked

✓ GROUPING LAYERS

If you want your Adjustment Layer to affect, say, two of the layers in your image, you can group them by clicking the **Create a New Group** button at the bottom of the Layers palette so it contains them in a folder. Click and drag the layers you want to group in to that folder, add your Adjustment Layer to the folder, too, and change the **Blend Mode** from **Pass Through** to **Normal**. The adjustment will only be applied to that group.

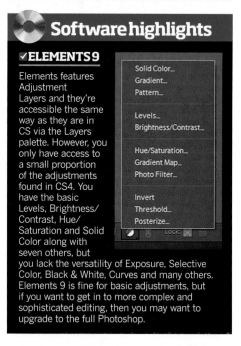

Software highlights

✓ ELEMENTS 9

Elements features Adjustment Layers and they're accessible the same way as they are in CS via the Layers palette. However, you only have access to a small proportion of the adjustments found in CS4. You have the basic Levels, Brightness/Contrast, Hue/Saturation and Solid Color along with seven others, but you lack the versatility of Exposure, Selective Color, Black & White, Curves and many others. Elements 9 is fine for basic adjustments, but if you want to get in to more complex and sophisticated editing, then you may want to upgrade to the full Photoshop.

HOW TO... SAVE LAYERED IMAGES

When you apply multiple layers to your image, be it image layers or Adjustment Layers, the size of your file will increase accordingly. To compress the image for printing or web use, once you're happy with the final edited image, go to *Layer>Flatten Image* to merge all the layers back in to the Background Layer. Then save the image as a JPEG or TIFF. It's a good idea to always keep a Photoshop version of your image (.PSD), which retains the various layers in your image, so that you have the option of re-editing the picture differently later if you need to.

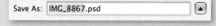

Using an Adjustment Layer with a Layer Mask

Learn how to selectively control the effects of an Adjustment Layer by 'painting' on a Layer Mask

1 Open your image in Photoshop and then duplicate the Background layer so you're working on a copy (*Layer>Duplicate Layer*). Now apply an *Adjustment Layer* of choice. Here we've chosen Hue/Saturation.

2 Make your necessary adjustments. We've boosted the colour in this portrait but, as you can see, it also make the skin tones very unnatural. We need to neutralise the colour on the face while retaining the saturation elsewhere.

3 Attached to the Adjustment Layer in the Layers palette is a Layer Mask, which looks like an empty white box. Click on it to make it active. Then select your *Brush Tool* from the toolbar, with a soft-edge medium-sized brush set to *Black*.

4 Using the *Brush Tool*, 'paint' over the areas of the image you want to revert back to their original state, varying the *Opacity* to control by how much. The Layer Mask turns black where you're painting. Use *White* paint to reverse the effect.

Three more ways for you to use an Adjustment Layer

For more precision editing, master these three techniques for improved results and added flexibility

1 REDUCE THE ADJUSTMENT
CONTROL THE EFFECT'S STRENGTH

However you apply an Adjustment Layer, you'll notice the full extent of its effect on your image instantly. Sometimes, though, this effect is too strong for the finish you want. An easy way to control the strength of the effect on the image is to reduce the *Opacity* of the Adjustment Layer. Once you've made your adjustments, select the Adjustment Layer so it's highlighted blue and drag the *Opacity* slider at the top of the Layers palette gradually down from 100% until you reach the desired strength.

2 BE SELECTIVE
MAKE LOCALISED ADJUSTMENTS

For a slightly more advanced but precise way to selectively apply an adjustment to an area of an image using an Adjustment Layer, simply create the selection and refine the edge (see pages 38-45 for more details on how to do this.) Here, we've used the Quick Selection Tool. Then apply the *Adjustment Layer* of choice. This instantly fills the attached Layer Mask with black, blocking any adjustments that you then might make in areas other than what you have selected.

3 CLIP LAYERS TOGETHER
APPLY TO ONLY CERTAIN LAYERS

Clipping an Adjustment Layer means that it affects only the layer directly beneath it in the Layers palette. It's handy if you have an image made up of multiple layers with separate components, but you want to apply an Adjustment Layer to only one of them. You can clip the layers together by either pressing the *Clip* button at the bottom of the Adjustments panel or by holding down *Alt* while you click on the line that separates the two layers in the Layers palette.

Layer Blend Modes

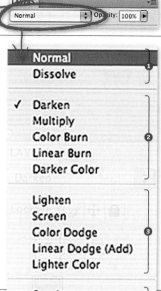

Along with Layers and Adjustment Layers, Blend Modes are essential parts of Photoshop's editing arsenal. Knowing how and when to use them can open a world of creative possibilities, especially when combined with Layer Masks

NOW YOU'VE GOT to grips with the principles of Layers and Adjustment Layers, it's a good place to introduce Blend Modes. They allow you to control how the content of a layer blends with the layer or layers directly below it. When you add a new layer to the Layers palette, by default the blending mode is set to Normal, which hides the lower layer with the content in the layer above it.

Without using a blending mode, the only way to merge layers together is to reduce the Opacity or Fill of any layer so the layer underneath shows through, but this alone doesn't yield very effective results.

There are 25 blending modes, which are all accessible from a drop-down menu at the top of the Layers palette, each affecting the way pixels interact. They're divided into six groups: Normal and Dissolve; Darken; Lighten;

Contrast; Comparative; and HSL. While we advise that you play about with all the modes to get a feel for their effects, in real editing terms there are only a dozen blending modes that a photographer might need to use on a regular basis for image editing. These are Darken, Multiply, Lighten, Screen, Overlay, Soft Light, Difference, Luminosity and Color.

You can apply a blending mode to any layer or Adjustment Layer. For instance, you could use Luminosity with an Adjustment Layer so it doesn't affect the colour components of the image. As a quick way to preview the effects of the various modes on an image, making sure the Brush Tool isn't selected, the Shift button can be held down and the + and – keys used to scroll up and down the list of blending modes.

FOUR BASIC WAYS TO USE BLEND MODES

To help you understand how blending modes work, here are four commonly used modes and ways to apply them to your images. Overlay superimposes the top layer on the base layer, while preserving the highlights and shadows of the bottom layer; Color replaces the hue and saturation of the base layer with the top layer; Darken replaces lighter pixels from the base layer with darker ones from the top layer; and Lighten is the opposite.

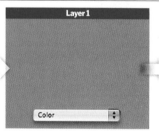

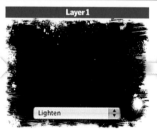

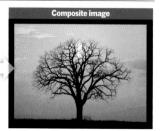

1) Normal and Dissolve: In Normal mode, the top layer is not affected by the layer beneath unless Opacity is less than 100%. The Dissolve mode turns some pixels of the top layer transparent.

2) Darken modes: Darken, Multiply, Color Burn, Linear Burn, Darker Color. These modes give prominence to dark-coloured pixels at varying degrees.

3) Lighten modes: Lighten, Screen, Color Dodge, Linear Dodge (Add), Lighter Color. These modes give prominence to light-coloured pixels for different effects.

4) Contrast modes: Overlay, Soft Light, Hard Light, Vivid Light, Linear Light, Pin Light and Hard Mix. These modes vary in strength when it comes to boosting your image's contrast.

5) Comparative modes: Difference and Exclusion. These modes create colours based on the difference between the top and base layer.

6) HSL modes: Hue, Saturation, Color, Luminosity. These modes replace the base layer pixels with the top layer pixels, depending on which mode is chosen.

Three ways Blend Modes can enhance your images

Here are a few ways of working with some of the most popular blending modes during photo editing

1 HIGH CONTRAST
USE IT TO DESATURATE

By blending a black & white image with a colour version using Hard Light, grey will be added to the resulting colour causing the image to become slightly desaturated. This mode also blends the colour from the base layer with the monochrome layer, darkening and lightening the shadows and highlights to boost the contrast.

2 APPLY TEXTURE
USE IT TO ADD INTEREST

Soft Light works in the same way as Hard Light and Overlay, but delivers much gentler results. By blending this image of wood over the top of the still-life image, the texture shows through subtly by darkening the blending pixels that are more than 50% grey and lightening those that are less than 50% grey.

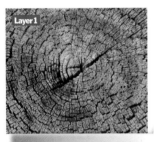

3 MERGING IMAGES
USE IT TO REPLACE A SKY

Multiply works by multiplying the base colour with the top colour to get the resulting colour. Every pixel gets darker, except for white, which remains unchanged. It's great for darkening overexposed areas and building up detail. Here, the white pixels are discarded and replaced with darker pixels, filling in the sky.

Levels

Boost the contrast and correct the colour of your images using one of the most popular adjustments in the Photoshop arsenal: Levels

LEVELS CONTROLS THE histogram, which holds all the exposure and colour detail in an image. Its primary role is to adjust the luminosity of a picture; its brightness, darkness, contrast and colour. It's a subset of Curves and a step up from Brightness/ Contrast, allowing for more precision in your adjustments. Levels is available as an image adjustment that directly affects an image's pixels (*Image>Adjustments*) or as an Adjustment Layer, which gives you the same experience, but is a veneer over the image. It's advisable to use the latter option whenever you can, as it's non-destructive and gives you the flexibility to edit and revisit changes at a later date, giving you a lot more creative control. You can select an Adjustment Layer from the Layers palette or by clicking *Layer>New Adjustment Layer*.

Via image menu

Via Layers menu

Via Layers palette

THE LEVELS DIALOGUE BOX

1) Auto The Auto function takes a look at the image and maps points from black to white to try to give the best tonal range.

2) Presets These functions are there to get you started quickly and easily, but while they work, they're not perfect. It's advisable to manually adjust the histogram using the sliders instead.

3) Histogram This black bumpy mound reflects the distribution of tones in your photograph. It shows the brightness range from dark to light and the peaks and troughs reflect how many pixels have that particular level of brightness. A well exposed image should have an even spread of peaks and troughs.

4) The eyedroppers The real power of Levels is in the three eyedroppers – they can set the black, mid-tone and the white point in the histogram, by clicking them on the darkest and lightest part of the image. The grey eyedropper also has the power to alter colour balance.

5) Input slider By far the most popular method of adjusting the histogram. Moving the three little triangles allows you to manually adjust the shadows, mid-tones and highlights to get a very balanced exposure.

6) Output levels Adjusts the output shadows and highlights. Leave this alone unless you deliberately want to adjust the output contrast, such as when working with a grayscale image.

7) Options Click to open the Auto Color Corrections Options dialogue box. It gives you different options for adjusting the colour in a less precise manner than the grey eyedropper, but it will go some way to correcting a colour cast.

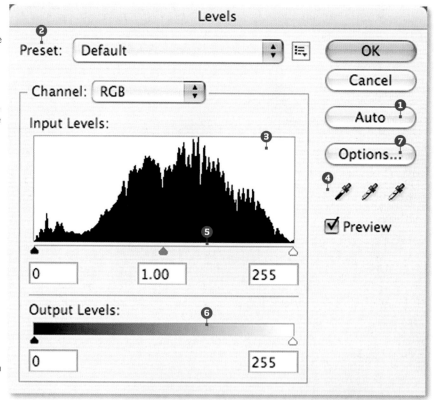

☑ LEVELS TIP: WHITE POINT

USE: PERFECT PRODUCT SHOTS

Product shots look great on a white backdrop, but more often than not – even if the image is correctly exposed – the backdrop can render as off-white or grey. Levels has a quick and easy way to correct this: using the white eyedropper, click on the greyest part of the background. This will turn it white, leaving the product relatively unaffected. Carefully adjust the midpoint and black sliders to bring any lost detail back in to the product. Great for eBay!

Secrets unlocked

☑ HIGHLIGHT WARNING

As you adjust the sliders, it can be easy to lose detail in either the highlights or shadows, known as clipping. To check for clipping, hold down *Alt* while clicking on the black or white slider triangle. The image will change to show a threshold view with hotspots that indicate where detail has been lost.

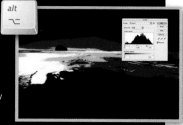

Three ways to use Levels

As you gain Photoshop experience and want to have more control over colour correction and contrast, different ways of applying the adjustments are available to suit your ability level and need for control

1 USE THE AUTO OPTION
ONE-CLICK AUTOMATIC RESULT

Once you open Levels, you'll be presented with a histogram. Pressing the **Auto** button is a good place to start as it takes a look at the image and maps points from black to white to get the best tonal range. A lot of the time, if you have an under or overexposed image, Auto will make it look a lot better. If you hold **Alt**, while clicking on **Auto**, the Auto Color Corrections Options dialogue box will appear, giving you options to adjust the colour balance.

2 EYEDROPPER
AUTOMATED WITH USER INVOLVEMENT

These can set a picture's tonal range by clicking on the image directly. To set black, click on the darkest area of the image with the black eyedropper. If it's lighter than any other part, you'll find the whole image will darken to compensate. The reverse happens with the white eyedropper if you do not select the lightest part of the image. The grey eyedropper selects the midpoint, but can also correct colour casts, depending on what neutral area you click on.

3 SLIDERS
FULL CONTROL FOR THE EXPERIENCED USER

On the Input Levels slider, you have three triangles: black for shadows; grey for Gamma, which controls the relative image brightness between the shadows and highlights; and white for the highlights. The idea is to move these triangles to expand the contrast without losing any detail in either the shadows or highlights (known as 'clipping'). The first thing to do is bring the black and white triangles in to align with the edges of the histogram – this will automatically move the Gamma slider, too. To intensify the highlights or shadows, move the **Gamma** slider and then use the grey eyedropper to correct any colour cast.

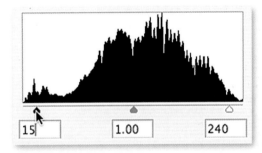

HOT KEY
Alt to reset

If you hold down **Alt**, the Cancel button in the dialogue box will change to Reset so you can revert back to the original image and start again. This will work for most of the dialogue boxes you use.

OPTIONS
Controlling colour

To access the Auto Color Correction Options in an Adjustment Layer, you need to click **Auto** while holding down **Alt**. To adjust the colour, click **Snap Neutral Midtones** and then experiment with the algorithms to find what works best.

CONNECT YOUR IMAGINATION

MANFROTTO 055 Tripod Series

Constantly imitated yet still unrivalled, the Manfrotto 055 tripod series offers an unparalleled combination of size, weight and stability. Consisting of seven professional standard tripods – three aluminium and four carbon fibre – the Manfrotto 055 tripod series has long set the standard of professional photographers.

Designed to offer a lightweight solution without compromising on precision and performance; features such as the patented Q90° system, levelling bubble, quick action leg locks and leg angle release mechanism complement the six models within the range ensuring that a solution exists for every photographer.

Q90° System –
Ideal for macro photography

Integrated Levelling Bubble –
Assist the accuracy of your shots

Manfrotto
Imagine More

manfrotto.co.uk

Curves

PC QUICK SELECT KEYS = ctrl M   MAC QUICK SELECT KEYS = ⌘ M

If you want more control over contrast, then get familiar with Curves and your images are sure to improve

CURVES IS PROBABLY the most powerful adjustment feature in Photoshop and also one of the most advanced, but once you've got to grips with it you'll find yourself using it time and time again. Just like Levels, Curves can be applied as an Adjustment or an Adjustment Layer (**Layer>Adjustment Layer>Curves**) and affects the tonal range of your image. Unlike Levels, you have far more control and many more features and methods of use – all of which could fill a book of their own – so we'll just be covering the basics here.

When you open the Curves adjustment panel, you'll be presented with a similar set-up to Levels but this time there's a diagonal line across the histogram: it's this line you'll need to move to adjust tonality. There are two adjustment points at either end of the line, which are the equivalent

to Level's Shadow and Highlight sliders. The additional control Curves offers comes from being able to click anywhere along this line to create as many adjustment points as you want to target specific areas of the histogram/tonal range. The whole idea behind using a curve is that tones are altered gradually, avoiding problems such as posterisation.

By moving the end points at the top and bottom, you also gain control of the darkest and lightest points of your image, which effectively does the same as the white and black Input and Output sliders in Levels. Pretty much everything you can do in Levels, you can do in Curves (although the reverse isn't true), so it's down to personal preference as to which you use for specific tasks, but Curves is definitely an upgrade in control.

How to create an 'S' curve

Using Curves can get complicated, but here's a useful technique that's highly effective and easy to do

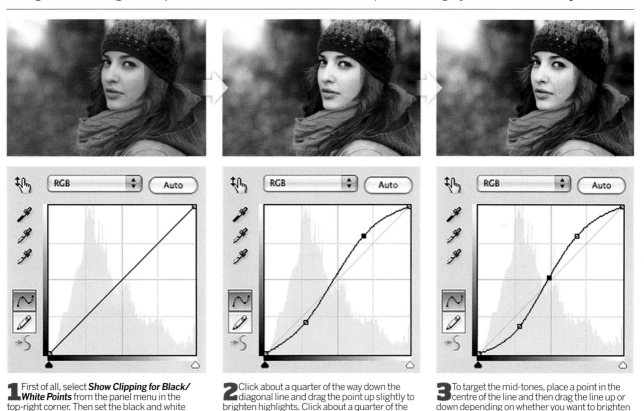

1 First of all, select **Show Clipping for Black/White Points** from the panel menu in the top-right corner. Then set the black and white points to the edges of the histogram as you would in Levels. Or hold down **Alt** as you drag the black or white **Input** sliders to preview the clipping.

2 Click about a quarter of the way down the diagonal line and drag the point up slightly to brighten highlights. Click about a quarter of the way up the line from the bottom and drag the point down to darken the shadows. The steeper the curve is, the stronger the contrast will be.

3 To target the mid-tones, place a point in the centre of the line and then drag the line up or down depending on whether you want to brighten or darken the mid-tones. You can change the colour of an image, too, using Curves, see *Secrets unlocked* below for more details.

Secrets unlocked

✓ TARGET MODE

Instead of manually adjusting the line in the Curves chart, click on the hand icon in the top left of the control panel. You can now click on an area of the image you want to adjust, and click and drag the cursor up (to brighten) or down (to darken) for more intricate control.

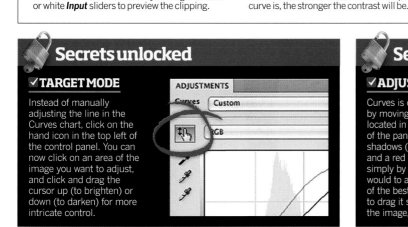

Secrets unlocked

✓ ADJUST THE CHANNELS

Curves is capable of adding colour casts by moving the individual colour channels, located in the drop-down menu at the top of the panel. You could add a blue cast to shadows (or remove one for that matter) and a red cast to highlights, for example, simply by moving the Curves line as you would to adjust the global contrast. One of the best ways to do this is to set a middle point on the curve and to drag it slightly up or down to add or reduce the colour channel in the image, respectively.

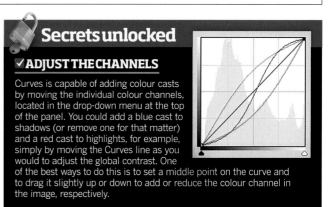

Dodge & Burn Tools

PC & MAC QUICK SELECT KEY
FOR PHOTOSHOP CS & ELEMENTS

   Brush: 100 ❶ | Range: Midtones ❷ | Exposure: 50% ❸ | ❹ | ☑ Protect Tones ❺ |

Sometimes you need to get a little more selective with your lightening and darkening. The Dodge & Burn Tools can give you ultimate control

MOST EXPOSURE ADJUSTMENTS target an image globally at first, but the Dodge and Burn Tools have the power to locally extend an image's tonal range, allowing you to be much more precise in the areas that you want to darken or lighten. They work particularly well on black & white images, but since CS4, there have been major improvements in the way the tools handle colour, too. It used to be that these tools caused a colour shift, but with the new Protect Tones command, this is kept to a minimum.

To get the best seamless adjustment with these tools, photographers should use them on small areas of an image, using a soft-edged brush, a low Exposure of below 10% and multiple strokes. Not doing these things means the exposure adjustment will look too harsh compared with the surrounding pixels, causing an outline around your adjusted area. If you want to make broader tonal adjustments over larger areas, we'd recommend using an Adjustment Layer and masking it off, which we'll explain how to do later. This has essentially the same effect as the Dodge and Burn Tools, but it's non-destructive. Unfortunately, any dodging or burning you do with the tools permanently alters the original pixels, so before you do any work with these tools, make sure you duplicate the image you're to work on first (*Layer>Duplicate Layer*).

❶ **Brush:** Select the *Size* and *Hardness* of your brush. It's always best to work with a very soft brush, so set the *Hardness* to *0-10%*.
❷ **Range:** Select the tonal range you want to target. Generally it's best to keep this set to *Midtones* when you dodge or burn.
❸ **Exposure:** Set the strength of the effect. It's best to start with a very low *Exposure* of *15%* and layer the effect.
❹ **Airbrush:** Builds the effect up based on how long you press your mouse or pen down for, not by how many strokes you take. Leave this off when dodging and burning.
❺ **Protect Tones:** Protects colour, highlights and shadows detail. Always have this activated.
❻ **Brush Palette:** A shortcut to accessing the complex brush panel. You don't need to worry about this too much – everything you need to start with is in Brush.

Dodge & Burn for landscapes

Master manipulating shadows and highlights in your landscapes

A classic darkroom technique that photographers have used for years, dodging and burning methods have never been as precise or controllable as they are in Photoshop. Before digital, you literally had to work in the dark, dodging and burning a sheet of photographic paper by blocking areas you wanted to over- or underexpose. You'd never know what it looked like until you developed the print. With Photoshop, the principles are the same, but you can be much more specific in where you darken or lighten, and even correct any mistakes you may make.

1 Pick your image. Here, the sky is a lot brighter than the foreground, both of which need attention to bring back detail. Open the image and create an editable *50% Gray layer* (see box, right).

2 Target the mid-tones for best results. So, for the Dodge and Burn Tools, set the *Range* to *Midtones* and use a medium-sized brush with a *Hardness* of *0%* and a low *Exposure* of between *5-20%*.

3 First, bring some of the cloud detail into the sky using the *Burn Tool*, lowering the *Exposure* if the whites turn grey. With the detail back, change the *Range* to *Shadow* to darken details if needed.

4 Switch to the *Dodge Tool* and brush over grey areas of the foreground to enhance the highlights or to brighten dark areas that have lost definition. Done right, this will increase contrast.

Secrets unlocked

☑ NON-DESTRUCTIVE WORKFLOW

As you have to work with the Dodge and Burn Tools directly on the image pixels, to make the adjustments non-destructive, create a new layer (*Layer>New*) and fill it with 50% Gray (*Edit>Fill>Content>50% Gray*). Then set the layer's *Blend Mode* to *Overlay*, so that the grey pixels are no longer visible. Now, with the grey layer selected, dodge and burn as you see fit. You'll find that the effects show on the original image, without affecting the original pixels. If you make a mistake and want to start again, simply delete the grey layer and no harm is done.

Software highlights

☑ CS5: TABLET PRESSURE

Selecting this will override any pressure sensitivity that you've set in the Brush Panel so you can control the size of the Dodge or Burn Tools via the pressure of your tablet's pen. You can find the function in the Options toolbar next to the Protect Tones feature.

Use the Dodge & Burn Tools for retouching portraits

These tools can be used to improve any picture. Here are three techniques to enhance your portraits

1 SKIN RETOUCHING
USE IT TO REDUCE WRINKLES

Professional photographers can't risk getting sloppy when retouching skin, especially if their images get blown up to the size of a billboard. Any hair, clogged pore or wrinkle can be seen at that scale, so there's no room for error. Instead of replacing pixels like the other retouching tools, the Dodge Tool retains the original skin texture, so you're reducing blemishes rather than getting rid of them, retaining the character of the face. Set the **Dodge Tool** to a low **Exposure** and brush over the areas you want to minimise. If it produces a colour shift, use the **Brush Tool** and sample a colour close to the area that's been retouched by pressing **Alt** (Mac) or **Cmd** (PC). Then brush over the area with the brush set to **Color Mode** to restore the correct tone.

2 HIDING A DOUBLE CHIN
USE IT TO MINIMISE SHADOWS

You're always better to reduce rather than eliminate elements in Photoshop to ensure a natural look. The Dodge and Burn Tools are great for this and can be particularly useful for reducing the appearance of a double chin by making it look like it's in shadow. It only works, though, if the portrait is taken front-on.

■ Use the **Burn Tool** with a low **Exposure** of around **10%**, **0% Hardness** and **Range** set to **Midtones**, then brush over the excess flesh to darken it gradually. Watch for any colour shift.

■ Switch to the **Dodge Tool** to reduce the appearance of any creases around the second chin to refine the jawline. You may need to increase the **Exposure** and use a smaller brush.

 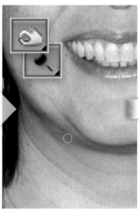 

3 WHITENING TEETH
USE IT FOR INSTANT BRIGHTENING

A bright smile can do wonders for enhancing your portraits, but there's a fine line between making coffee-stained teeth look natural white and glow in the dark, so be careful.

■ To whiten a person's teeth, set the **Dodge Tool** to an **Exposure** of about **20%** and the **Range** to **Midtones**, then paint over each tooth to brighten them, being careful not to overdo it. For the back teeth, which naturally won't be as bright as the front, switch the **Range** to **Shadows** and brush over them to make them slightly lighter.

■ Use a brush that's a little smaller than the area you want to work on and, for the best results, brush from the inside of the area and work your way out to the edges so it blends well.

 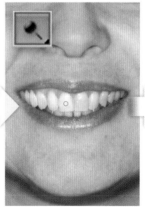 

SUB TOOL: SPONGE TOOL

USE: SELECTIVE SATURATION

The Sponge Tool, found underneath the Dodge and Burn Tools in the toolbar, can be used to locally decrease or increase colour saturation.
Like a brush, you can adjust the Size and Hardness of the sponge; normally the softer it is, the smoother the results will be. You can also change the strength by altering the **Flow** and switch from **Saturate** to **Desaturate** via the **Mode** option.

Secrets unlocked

✓ NEW WINDOW

Click **Window>Arrange> New Window for [filename]** to create a shadow image. Now you can zoom into the working image and have the shadow image open to see the overall effect, saving you from zooming in and out, and making your editing easier.

HOT TIP

The default Exposure setting for the Dodge and Burn Tool is normally 50% and this is way too strong. Reduce this to no more than **20%** for most of your work and gradually build up the exposure.

Exposure: 20%

Black & White...

Learn how to take control over your black & white conversions to maximise detail, tonal range and creative effect

THERE'S NO DENYING that colour can be beautiful, but black & white is often classic, elegant and can be very powerful with the right kind of scene or subject. It's a favourite with most photographers, whether of the film or digital age, as we can all appreciate its compelling charisma. So, how can you craft a tonally rich black & white image post-capture?

When working with film, photographers used to rely on colour filters to modify a scene's tonal range: for modest adjustments, they'd use the yellow or orange filter; and for a dramatic difference, a red filter. A red filter lightens every red tone in the scene and darkens everything else. It was very popular with portrait photographers as it lightened skin tones, and with landscape photographers as it made blue skies darker and more dramatic.

In essence, this is how a Black & White adjustment layer works: once you apply the Adjustment Layer (*Layer>New Adjustment Layer>Black & White...*) the image will instantly be converted to mono. You'll be faced with a dialogue box that allows you to adjust the various colours in the image to improve and control the tonal range, the same way you would when applying a colour filter to your camera.

The fact it's an Adjustment Layer means any alterations you make are non-destructive, you can delete or edit the layer at any time, and it gives you precise control over the colour channels. Above all, though, it's one of the easiest, most versatile and quickest routes to turning a colour image into a punchy black & white masterpiece.

Secrets unlocked

☑ TARGET MODE

Rather than use the sliders, if you click on the Hand Tool in the top of the dialogue box, you can click on any area of the image to target a specific colour that you want to modify. Then, when the hand cursor appears, click and drag it left or right to decrease or increase its strength.

NAVIGATING THE MENU

1) Preset: Select a predefined grayscale mix or a previously saved grayscale mix.

2) Target mode: Use this optional tool with an Adjustment Layer to make changes directly on an image (see box, left). It's an automatic facility with *Image>Adjustments*.

3) Tint: Check this box and select a colour to add a duotone tint to your picture.

4) Auto: Sets a grayscale mix based on the image's colour values. Use it as a starting point, then tweak the tone using the colour sliders.

5) Colour channels: These sliders affect the grayscale tone of each colour in the picture.

6) Clip: Use this to link the adjustment layer to the layer/s beneath it to limit its effect. It's useful if you're working with multiple layers but don't want to affect them all.

7) Reset: Click this icon to revert all the sliders back to their default position.

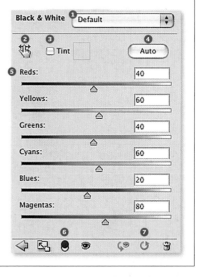

☑ TRY USING...
BLEND MODES WITH A BLACK & WHITE ADJUSTMENT LAYER

You can change the tone and contrast of your colour image using Blend Modes.

By applying a Black & White adjustment layer and then using a Blend Mode to control how the layer interacts with the colours of the original image beneath, you can get some interesting and appealing results. The three key Blend Modes worth looking at are Soft Light and Overlay for contrast, and Luminosity for colour. If the effect is too strong, you can simply reduce the opacity of the Black & White adjustment layer. The beauty of doing this is that you can adjust the brightness of the image's individual colours by moving the Adjustment Layer's colour sliders.

Overlay: Boosts the contrast of a colour image by darkening and lightening tones.

Soft Light: Has a gentler but similar effect to Overlay blend mode.

Luminosity: This mode allows you to adjust the luminance and brightness of each colour without altering the saturation.

HOT TIP

Black & White in Elements 9

Duplicate the original layer and go to *Enhance>Convert to Black & White* and pick the conversion preset you want to use. You can then adjust the intensity of the tones using the Red, Green, Blue and Contrast colour sliders.

HOT KEY

Hide layer

To temporarily view your image before your previous change in the Adjustment Layer, hold down the \ key. It's a useful way to see how your latest adjustment affected your image.

Three ways to use Black & White on your images

The Black & White adjustment layer can be used for more than just a simple monochrome conversion. Read on to find out how to selectively colour and tint your image with the help of a Layer Mask

1 TURN AN IMAGE BLACK & WHITE
LEARN TO CONTROL THE TONALITY OF YOUR MONOCHROME CONVERSION

To convert a colour image to black & white, first go to *Layer> New Adjustment Layer>Black & White...* or access the Adjustment shortcut from the b&w circle icon at the bottom of the Layers palette. Your image will instantly turn black & white. Now click *Auto*; this will create a fairly accurate tonal conversion that you can then refine to your liking later. Alternatively, select one of the filters or effects from the *Preset* drop-down menu. Either way, once you have a basic conversion, use the colour sliders to target individual grayscale tones. At this point, it may help to flick back to your original image to judge the colours you want to refine by clicking the *eye* icon, next to the Adjustment Layer in the Layers palette.

2 TINT AN IMAGE USING BLACK & WHITE
CREATE A DUOTONE PHOTOGRAPH

Before you tint your picture, use a *Black & White* adjustment layer to get the contrast you want. Then create a new *Black & White* adjustment layer and clip it to the Adjustment Layer beneath it, so you've created one Adjustment Layer for your b&w conversion and another for tinting, which comes in useful later. Check the *Tint* box and double-click on the coloured box next to it to open the colour picker. Once you've selected the coloured tint you want by using the gradient or colour library, you may find that the colour is too strong for your picture and you want to reduce the cast. As you're working on a new Adjustment Layer, you can reduce the layer's *Opacity* by moving the slider in the Layers palette to tone down the effect without revealing the original image underneath, as you would do normally.

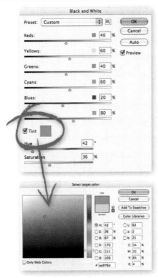

3 SELECTIVE COLOURING USING BLACK & WHITE
ADD IMPACT TO YOUR MONO PICTURES

Convert your image to black & white. Then add a Layer Mask to the Adjustment Layer by clicking *Layer>Layer Mask*. At this point, decide if you want most of your image colour with a touch of black & white or a black & white picture with a touch of colour, and then pick *Hide All* or *Reveal All*, respectively. Here, Reveal All was used as the majority will be black & white. Now select the *Brush Tool* and set the paint colour to *Black*. With the Layer Mask selected, paint over the area you want to turn to colour using a soft brush that's smaller than the area you're painting. If you make a mistake, switch the paint colour to *White* and zoom in to the image for more precision and paint the areas you want to return to b&w. To delete the Layer Mask, click the grey link on the Adjustment Layer and drag the Layer Mask in to the trash at the bottom of the Layers palette.

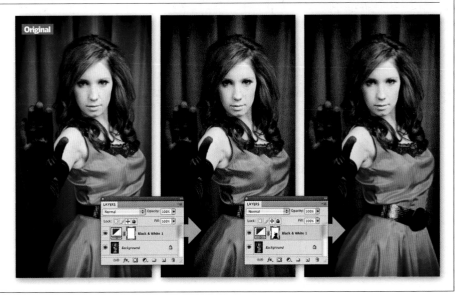

Hue/Saturation

Avoid lacklustre or overcooked colours by learning how to improve vibrancy, change hues and control the saturation of specific channels

PHOTOSHOP HAS LITERALLY dozens of ways to allow you to alter colour, but one of the most powerful methods – and also one that's often overlooked – is Hue/Saturation. It's rarely exploited to its fullest, yet it enables you to eliminate colour casts, make colours appear richer and more vibrant, and improve the overall tonality of an image. You can also make adjustments globally or selectively by targeting a narrow range of colours. Turn an image black & white by dragging the Saturation slider to the left, or tint your image using the Colorize option.

Like most adjustments, Hue/Saturation can be accessed via the ***Image>Adjustments*** menu, but we'd always advise using an adjustment layer (***Layer>New Adjustment Layer>Hue/Saturation***) for more flexibility. While you have the same controls in both, the former option applies colour changes directly to an image's pixels so, for one, it can be destructive to an image, and two, if you make a mistake you may have to start all over again by deleting the image layer if you can't step far enough back in the History panel; undoing any other adjustments you've made to the image. The beauty of an adjustment layer is that you can make the same changes without directly affecting the original image. Instead, when you make a mistake, you can simply delete the adjustment layer – and, best of all, it is fully editable so you can undo or make further changes at any point during the editing process.

You can adjust the hue and saturation in Adobe Camera Raw, found under the HSL/Grayscale tab, as well as the luminance of eight different colour ranges independently, but you'll need to convert it to a Smart Object by holding down **Shift** and pressing **OK** to make it non-destructive and editable later.

NAVIGATING THE MENU

1) Preset: With one click, you can boost the overall saturation of specific colours and tint your image sepia or cyanotype.

2) Master: Access specific colours so you can make targeted adjustments.

3) Hue: Drag this slider to the left or right to change the colours (hue) of your image. The bar of rainbow colours will tell you the colour range you're applying. Colours black, white and grey remain unchanged.

4) Saturation: Use this slider to control the intensity of the colours. Drag it to the left to drain the image of all colour and to the right to increase its impact to unnatural proportions.

5) Lightness: Control the brightness of your image. Drag the slider to the left to make it darker and to the right to make it lighter.

6) Colorize: With this option selected, you can use the Hue slider to apply a global tint to your image. It works well if you desaturate your image first by dragging the **Saturation** slider to the far left.

7) Preview: View how changes affect the image.

8) Eyedroppers: Use to select a specific colour to target or to add or subtract from the colour range.

9) Colour range: This bar denotes what colours are in the range that you are targeting. To narrow or expand the range, adjust the half triangles.

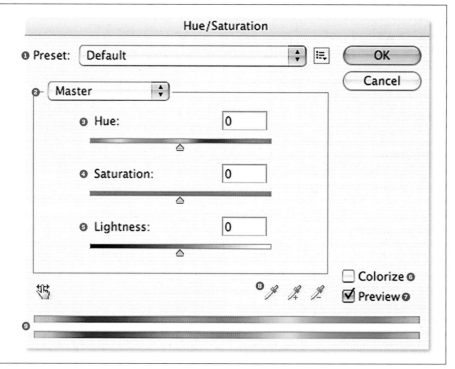

⚠ WARNING: KEEP IT REAL!

When adjusting the hue, try to keep to the colours either side of your source colour. If you make the change too dramatic it won't look natural, and you could get an unsightly halo and artifacts. It's the same with the saturation: be watchful that the colours don't become too vibrant, as they'll look overprocessed and you may find you lose detail as the colour tones merge together.

☑ ALSO TRY... AUTO CORRECTIONS

The Auto Color command, found under the Image menu, is the most sophisticated Auto command and the easiest way to get rid of a colour cast. Normally it's advisable to avoid these commands as they offer no control, but if your image only needs minor tweaks, it can be a one-click wonder.

It works by taking an average reading of the dark and light pixels to determine what should be white and black, and then adjusts the colours appropriately. If you do try it, be sure to duplicate the image layer first (***Layer>Duplicate Layer***) so you're not working on the original image. This way if it doesn't work, you can simply delete the layer and no harm's done.

☑ ALSO TRY... VIBRANCE ADJUSTMENTS

The Vibrance command (***Layer>New Adjustment Layer>Vibrance***) is more relative than Saturation. When you boost an image's saturation you may find that shades of a colour all start to look the same. Vibrance will try to keep the relationship between the shades and therefore retain more detail.

However, you can't make selective adjustments with Vibrance; it affects the image globally. The command does work in a slightly different way, though, by only targeting the pixels that are the least saturated, and it protects skin tones so you can avoid giving your subjects an orange tan like you would with Saturation.

Uses for Hue/Saturation

Learn how to be specific with your colour adjustments with these two basic techniques for improving the impact of your pictures

1 HOW TO REMOVE A COLOUR CAST

USE HUE TO CORRECT WHITE BALANCE IN AN IMAGE

You can get a colour cast by setting the wrong White Balance for the lighting, like Daylight WB in a room full of fluorescent lights, or if your subject stands near a coloured surface that's reflecting light. While there are several ways to remove it in Photoshop, this is one of the easiest. Open the image and apply a *Hue/Saturation* adjustment layer, then select the colour of the tint that you want to get rid of from the drop-down menu at the top of the dialogue box. Slowly adjust the *Hue* slider to neutralise the cast and move the *Saturation* slider to the left to dull down the cast.

2 SELECTIVE COLOUR ADJUSTMENTS

TARGET A SPECIFIC COLOUR

Choose the colour you want to target from the drop-down menu at the top of the adjustment dialogue box. You'll find it selects every part of the image that contains part of that colour. If this hasn't selected every tone you want to target, or it's selected more than you wanted to adjust, you can use the eyedroppers in the top of the dialogue box to add or subtract from the colour range by clicking on the areas of the image you want to add or subtract. Finally, make your changes by altering the *Hue* or *Saturation* sliders, but be careful that you don't change the colours to the point that they look unnatural.

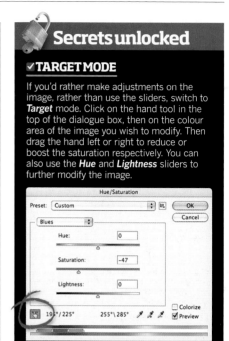
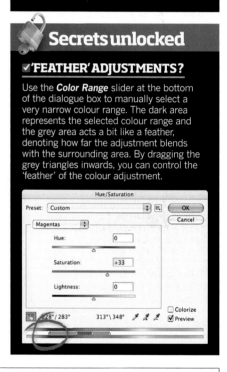
Working with a Hue/Saturation Adjustment Layer

Get more control over how an Adjustment Layer interacts with an image layer by using Blend Modes

One of the added benefits of working with an Adjustment Layer, like Hue/Saturation, is that you can control how that adjustment blends with the image layer beneath it. First, add the adjustment layer by clicking on the b&w symbol at the bottom of the Layers palette. Now use the drop-down menu at the top of the Layer palette to switch the *Blend Mode* from *Normal* (default) to 24 different options for different effects – have a play to see the different results. Color mode is the most suitable for the Hue/Saturation adjustment layer. It preserves the luminance of the image but replaces the hue and saturation of the Adjustment Layer. Often when you make colour adjustments the brightness is also affected, but using this Blend Mode avoids this happening.

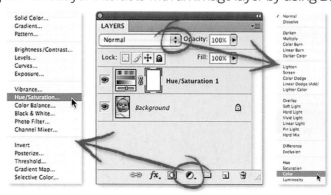

HOT TIP

Clipping Mask
If you only want an adjustment layer to affect a single layer, you can go to *Layer>Create Clipping Mask* and that will limit the effect of the Hue/Saturation layer to only the layer beneath it.

Using selection tools

The various selection tools available in Photoshop vary in difficulty and control, but are generally used for the same purpose: to copy areas of an image and for making localised adjustments. Find out how...

MAKING A SELECTION is fairly easy: some tools require you to draw around an area while others are 'smarter', deciding how much of an area is selected based on its tonal range and colour. The tricky part comes from making a clean selection, so that the edges of the selection blend with the rest of the image. When the edges of a selection are not manipulated correctly, it can ruin a picture and make it look amateurish. Every photographer wants to achieve a seamless finish, whereby the viewer cannot tell what parts of an image have been tweaked or added and what parts are original. Increasingly, photographers are 'compositing' images together, which can range from copying a few extra people into a scene to bulk out a crowd or swapping a dull sky for a dramatic one, to creating a whole image from dozens of different pictures, which can become very advanced and complex. The key to making images like this look realistic and straight off-camera is seamless selections. We recommend when doing any Photoshop work, especially when making selections, to invest in a pen tablet like Wacom's Bamboo or Intuos 4, as, with practice, it will become a lot easier and more precise than using a mouse.

The main selection tools available in Photoshop CS5 and Elements 10 are the Marquee, Lasso, Magic Wand and Quick Selection tools, but you can also use a brush in conjunction with CS5's Quick Mask Mode or Element's Selection Brush. Whatever tool you use, once you make a selection you'll end up with a flashing dotted line that's often referred to as 'marching ants' to denote your selection. You'll then be able to control and refine your selection by using features under the Select menu or in the Options toolbar, which allows you to adjust the smoothness of your edges, among other things.

Marquee tools

PC & MAC QUICK SELECT KEY — M
FOR PHOTOSHOP CS & ELEMENTS

   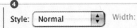

Find out how to make and combine shape-based selections and create accent features like borders and vignettes using the marquee tools

THE MOST BASIC set of selection tools to use, but not the most precise or controllable, are the marquee tools. They comprise the Rectangular, Elliptical, Single Row and the Single Column Marquee Tool, which work by creating rectangular and oval shapes. While they may seem only applicable to standard-shaped selections, you can use the tools for more advanced selections by making and combining more than one shape. For instance, if you want to select a slither of a moon, you could create one circle and, holding down *Alt* to subtract from the selection, create another circle within it for a half-moon shape. You can also use these tools to create borders or, when combined with a large feather and Levels adjustment, a vignette.

❶ **Selection mode:** New selection, Add to selection, Subtract from selection and Intersect with selection (left to right).
❷ **Feather:** Softens the edges of selections.
❸ **Anti-alias:** Allows for a smooth edge transition. You should keep this switched on.
❹ **Style:** Sets how the tool draws.
❺ **Refine Edge:** This becomes active once you've made an initial selection.

1 Select the marquee tool that you want to use from the toolbar. Here, we used the Rectangular Marquee Tool as it's the best suited to select the inside of the window frame.

2 To make the selection, click and drag the cursor into the shape you need. If you're not happy with the selection's position, click on its centre and drag it to where you want it.

HOT TIP

While dragging a marquee tool, hold down the *spacebar* (do not release the mouse) to move the undefined selection. Release the *spacebar* and continue dragging.

HOT KEY

Caps Lock

To help with your selections, click *Caps Lock* to display the tool's cursor in precise mode.

HOT KEY esc

Escape

If you make a selection and then click in the wrong place or on the canvas so your selection disappears, press the *Esc* key to make your selection reappear.

3 To make multiple selections, like we've done here, hold down *Shift* while creating another selection. Try combining selections or pressing *Alt* to subtract from a selection.

Secrets unlocked

☑ **TRANSFORM SELECTIONS**

Once you've made your selection using any of the selection tools, you can adjust its shape, size and rotation. If it's a little too big or a little too small, you can resize the selection marquee by going to *Select>Transform Selection*. See page 18 for more details on Transform commands.

Similar

Transform Selection

Edit in Quick Mask Mode

Lasso tools

PC & MAC QUICK SELECT KEY = **L**
FOR PHOTOSHOP CS & ELEMENTS

 ① ② ③ ⑥ | Feather: 0 px | ☑ Anti-alias | Width: 10 px | Contrast: 10% | Frequency: 57 | ⑦ | ⑤ Refine Edge...

Find out how to get the most from the versatile and precise Lasso tools and what you should consider when picking the right tool for the job

FOR MORE CONTROL over your selection and freeform shapes, the Lasso tools enable you to draw around an area to create a selection. It requires some eye-to-hand coordination to use these tools and they're better suited to smaller subjects. Many people who use these tools start selecting an area, mess it up, give up and start again, instead of continuing with the selection and refining it afterwards. Once you've completed your selection, you can hold the **Shift** key and draw in extra areas to add to the selection or, with the **Alt** key pressed, subtract from it. If you want to apply a feather to your selection, you must do this before you make a selection, or otherwise wait until after and make adjustments using the Refine Edge function.

> ① to ⑤ **See marquee tools' description.**
> ⑥ **Width, Contrast & Frequency:** *(Magnetic Lasso Tool only)* Set the distance you need to be from the edge to select it, the level of edge contrast and the frequency of anchor points added as you draw the path.
> ⑦ **Use tablet pressure:** Click this button to be able to control the width of the tablet's pen.

LASSO TOOL
IDEAL FOR: AREAS WHERE PRECISION IS LESS IMPORTANT

A freeform tool that gives you complete control over your selection, the Lasso Tool is not ideal for objects with straight edges as it requires an extremely steady hand. To make a selection, click on a starting point and draw around the area you want to select, without releasing the mouse, until you finish at the point you started at. If you release the mouse too early, Photoshop will finish the selection for you by drawing a straight line back to the starting point. You can create a straight line by holding down the **spacebar**.

MAGNETIC LASSO TOOL
IDEAL FOR: OBJECTS A DIFFERENT COLOUR FROM THE BACKDROP

The most versatile tool of the set as it's designed to recognise areas of different tonal contrast and can follow the contours of a complicated shape. The tool attempts to detect the outline of an object and places anchor points along its edge: for complicated shapes, increase the **Frequency** value in the Option toolbar. If you find it goes a little astray, press the delete button to get rid of the last anchor point and start the section again, creating more anchor points this time to control the selection.

POLYGONAL LASSO TOOL
IDEAL FOR: STRAIGHT EDGES AND ULTIMATE CONTROL

The Polygonal Lasso Tool enables you to draw poker-straight lines around a subject. Each time you want to change the line's direction, you need to click the mouse. Photoshop won't finish the selection for you, so you have to make as many straight lines as needed to return to the point you started at. You can make complicated selections by making several small lines.

Tools of the trade

☑ USING A GRAPHICS TABLET

Making selections can be made much easier with a pressure-sensitive graphics tablet such as Wacom's Bamboo or Intuos 4 (the latter is for the advanced users in need of more control over their editing). With practice, they're easier and more versatile than a mouse as they're ergonomically better for drawing. You can also assign shortcuts to different pressure points on the pen such as brush size and feather.
For details, visit: www.wacom.eu

HOW DO I...
Deselect a crop?
To undo your selection, click outside the marching ants using a different selection tool or by clicking **Select>Deselect** (**Cmd** & **D** for Mac or **Ctrl** & **D** for PC).

HOT TIP
Switching between tools
If you hold down the shortcut key for a tool and press **Shift** you can flick through the subtools. Press **W** for Magic Wand, **M** for Marquee and **L** for Lasso first, and use **Shift** to access the Quick Selection or Magnetic Lasso Tool, for example.

Brush Tool

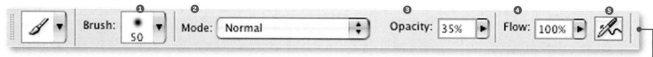

Access the hidden secrets of the Brush Tool and find out how it can help you retouch and selectively adjust your image's colour, exposure and contrast

THE BRUSH TOOL has some of the most diverse and useful applications for post-processing images. Designed to replicate the effect of a paintbrush, the tool's primary purpose is to apply colour to an image specified via clicking on the colour palette at the bottom on the toolbar. But it has many more sophisticated uses than just 'painting' colour on a canvas – for example, you can use it to edit the tonality of pictures by using it in conjunction with a Layer Mask, to retouch pictures and skin tones and to make selections (see page 22 for more details).

The Brush Tool's options are overwhelming, especially in CS5. While you can alter the shape, size and style of your brush in CS4, as well as the Flow and Opacity of the paint, in CS5 you also have more bristle-tip types to choose from to improve your control, accuracy and creative potential. You can select various types of flat and round brushes as well as setting parameters like how thick and long each bristle is, depending on the type of brush stroke you want to replicate, and the wetness and paint load. As a photographer who is really only interested in editing their pictures, on a day-to-day basis you'll probably only graze the surface of the Brush Tool's potential and have little need to even access the crammed Brush Panel (see below) for the advanced parameters. The options, however, are well worth exploring in case you fancy getting into digital art or want to apply a creative design to one of your pictures.

❶ **Brush palette:** Selects the size, shape, texture and hardness of your brush to suit your adjustment.
❷ **Mode:** Determines how pixels in the image are affected by the Brush Tool and its paint.
❸ **Opacity:** Controls the density of the paint and its level of coverage.
❹ **Flow:** Controls the liquidity of the paint and the speed it's applied.
❺ **Airbrush:** When switched on, you can build the paint up depending on how long you hold your mouse or pen down for, not by how many strokes you take.

THE BRUSH PANEL

While shortcuts and the Options panel will usually quickly provide you with the brush you need, if you want to explore your control over the Brush Tool, look towards the Brush Panel. To open it, go to **Window>Brushes** or right-click **Ctrl** and click on the image, and you'll be able to change the tip's style, as well as other more detailed settings such as preset shapes and textures. Rarely would a photographer need this much power – it's intended more for digital artists – but if you get into creative painting and digital illustrations, it's worth checking out.

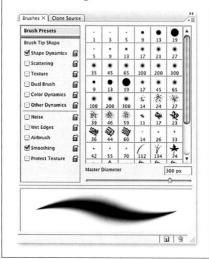

BRUSH TOOL BLEND MODES

1) Normal: This is the default mode. It paints/edits each pixel to turn the base colour (the layer you're applying it to) in to the blend colour (the colour loaded on the brush).

2) Behind: Paints/edits only on transparent areas of an image. It only works on layers that have Lock Transparency deselected.

3) Clear: Paints/edits pixels to make them transparent, similar to an eraser. It only works on layers that have Lock Transparency deselected.

4) Soft Light: Darkens or lightens the base colour, depending on what blend colour is used. The effect is similar to shining a diffused light on the image. If the brush's colour is lighter than 50% grey, the image is lightened as if it were dodged. If the brush's colour is darker than 50% grey, the image is darkened as if it were burned in. Painting with pure black or white produces a distinctly darker or lighter area, but does not result in pure black or white, and other colours will leave a light tint on the image.

5) Hue: Creates a resulting colour from the luminance and saturation of the base colour combined with the hue of the blend colour.

6) Saturation: Creates a resulting colour from the luminance and hue of the base colour combined with the saturation of the blend colour.

7) Color: Creates a result colour with the luminance of the base colour and the hue and saturation of the blend colour. This is useful if you want to turn part of an image black & white or you're tinting an image.

8) Luminosity: Creates a result colour with the hue and saturation of the base colour and the luminance of the blend colour. This mode creates the inverse effect of Color mode.

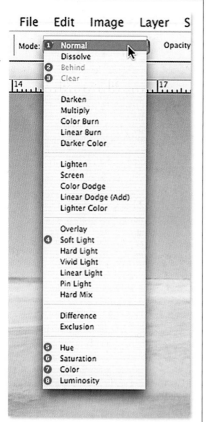

HOT KEY

Brackets
Brushes can be accessed via the Options bar or via **Window>Brushes**. However, if you're working on an image, and want to alter the brush's Size, press the right or the left square brackets (next to the letter P).

Secrets unlocked

■ History Brush Tool   Y
  Art History Brush Tool   Y

✔ HISTORY & ART HISTORY BRUSH

The History Brush Tool can be used to partially undo any adjustment, filter or tool. With the tool selected, click on the History Panel (**Window>History**) and click in the box next to the step you want to revert back to. This will select it as your source state. Now you can go back to the image and paint selectively to take the area back to the reverted state. You can go back as far as the History Panel allows: the default is 20 states but you can extend this via the **Preferences>General panel**. The Art History Brush works in a similar way but has the power to add an Impressionist look to your picture, similar to CS5's Mixer Brush and Element's Impressionist Brush. The biggest mistake people make with this tool is using too large of a brush so the edges blur and diminish detail.

HOT KEY

Number keys
To alter the paint's opacity, press **4** for **40%**, 7 for **70%** etc, unless you're working with the airbrush, in which case this affects the Flow. Hold **Shift** and press a number to affect the opacity of the airbrush.

Uses for the Brush Tool

Learn how to correct skin tones and reduce blemishes in portraits.
Plus we show you an easy way to correct problems with exposure

1 SKIN RETOUCHING
USE IT TO EVEN OUT SKIN TONE

An easy way to get rid of dark bags, or
to reduce wrinkles and blemishes, is to
take a sample of skin tone and paint it
over the area with a low-opacity brush. It's
always better to gradually build the colour
up to the tone you want with multiple
brush strokes.

■ Zoom in to the image so you have a
close-up view of the area you want to
retouch. Select a medium-sized brush
(no bigger than the area you're planning to
retouch), with a *Hardness* of around *0-10%*,
and the *Opacity* set to around *10%*.

■ Hold down the *Alt* key (Mac) or *Cmd*
(PC) so the brush cursor turns into an
eyedropper, then click on an area of colour
near the area you want to retouch. This
loads the colour on the brush. Now brush
over the area to even out the skin tone.
Take a new colour sample from next to
each area you retouch to ensure the
colours are similar in tone.

2 TONAL ADJUSTMENTS
USE IT TO CORRECT EXPOSURES

If parts of an image are under- or
overexposed, there's an easy,
non-destructive way to selectively
correct ill-exposed areas with the help of
the Brush Tool and Layer Masks. This
technique can be applied to contrast or
colour changes by simply using a different
adjustment layer.

■ Add an Exposure adjustment layer
(*Layer>New Adjustment Layer>Exposure*)
and adjust the sliders until the area you
want to amend is correctly exposed.

■ Each Adjustment Layer has a Layer
Mask attached. Select the mask, then set
the *Foreground color* to *Black* and pick a
soft, round brush with an *Opacity* of
100%. Paint over the area that's now
poorly exposed to bring back the detail
from the original image.

■ If you make a mistake, switch the
Foreground color to *White* and brush the
area back in on the Layer Mask.

Software highlights

☑ SPECIALITY BRUSHES

While the Brush Tool in Elements 9 and 10
works in the same way as in CS4, it also
offers speciality brushes that paint shapes
like stars, flowers and butterflies. Elements
9 also features the Impressionist Brush that
blurs and blends the edges of the objects
in your image to resemble an Impressionist
painting. It's tricky to get a handle on, but it
can yield interesting results. Try using it on
a duplicate layer and then reduce the layer's
opacity to see what happens.

☑ SMART BRUSH TOOL

While this brush can be used to make
selections in Elements 9 and 10, like the
Quick Selection Tool, it also edits your
image. Found underneath the Paint Brush
Tool, you can use it to make selective
adjustments by brushing over an area to
change the colour, adjust the exposure,
apply special effects or convert it to black
& white among other Smart Paint options.

☑ MIXER BRUSH IN CS5

This ingenious tool is designed to work
like an actual paintbrush, with a variety
of bristle tips, the ability to adjust the
amount of paint loaded on the brush and its
wetness – the same way you'd work if you
were applying paint to a real canvas. The
real showstopper is the Mixer Brush, which
enables you to literally mix the colours
in your photograph by controlling its Mix
value and Wetness. It takes practice, so don't
be discouraged if your picture looks like a
five-year-old's finger painting rather than a
Rembrandt masterpiece at first.

Tools of the trade

☑ USING A GRAPHICS TABLET

A Wacom tablet is really handy when
using the Brush Tool as brush movements
are much more natural. You can also
adjust the Opacity and the Size of the brush
based on your pressure points. If your
tablet's pen has barrel rotation, you can also
change the angle of your brush intuitively
rather than have to specify the angle in the
brush palette.

The Brush Tool and Layer Masks

Find out how painting on Layer Masks can be used to hide or reveal image information

By adding a Layer Mask to a layer
(*Layer>Layer Mask>Reveal All/Hide
All*), be it an image layer or an
Adjustment Layer, you can use the
Brush Tool to mask off areas of an image
so it's not affected by an adjustment.

For example, set the brush's colour to
Black, and select the Layer Mask, then
brush over the adjusted areas that you
want to hide.

White paint does the reverse and grey
partially does both, leaning towards one
or the other depending on how dark or
light the tone is. The process is
non-destructive; delete the Layer Mask
to undo any edits.

HOT TIP

You can download a
variety of brushes
from www.adobe.
com or from the web
for free. Then add
them to your Brush
Panel by clicking on
the small arrow in
the top-right corner
to access a
drop-down menu,
then clicking *Load
Brushes* to save
them to your palette.
Under the same
menu you'll also find
different pre-loaded
brush types that you
can add to your
palette.

Magic Wand Tool

PC & MAC QUICK SELECT KEY — W
FOR PHOTOSHOP CS & ELEMENTS

Got an area of a specific tone you want to select? Find out how the Magic Wand Tool can help you do this easily with seamless results

THE MAGIC WAND TOOL selects pixels of a similar colour to the area you click with the tool. The area of similarity can be expanded or contracted by making the Tolerance level (located in the Options toolbar) bigger or smaller respectively. You can expand your chosen area by also making multiple selections, holding down the **Shift** key and clicking on the areas you want to select, while altering the **Tolerance**. If you select **Contiguous** in the Options toolbar, you'll also only target pixels of the same colour that are connected to the area you click. You may find you get better results switching between the Magic Wand Tool and the Quick Selection Tool.

❶ **Selection mode:** New selection, Add to selection, Subtract from selection and Intersect with selection (left to right).
❷ **Tolerance:** Set range of colours.
❸ **Anti-alias:** Allows for a smooth edge transition. You should keep this switched on.
❹ **Contiguous:** Only select connected pixels.
❺ **Sample All Layers:** Sample colours from composite image.
❻ **Refine Edge:** This becomes active once you've made an initial selection.

1 The default setting of the Tolerance level is set to 32. If this only picks up a small area, as it did in this picture, increase the **Tolerance** to **50** for a better selection.

2 Increasing the Tolerance further may select parts of the image you don't want it to (in this case, the statue): to get around this, hold down **Shift** and click again to add to the selection.

HOT KEYS

Hide selection
To temporarily hide your selection and to see what adjustments you've made without deselecting your area, click **Cmd+H** (Mac) or **Ctrl+H** (PC). Press the key combination again to reveal the selection.

HOT TIP

Move selection
Once you've made your selection using one of the Lasso tools, click on the **Move Tool** to cut it from the image. At this point you may want to click and drag it on to another image to copy the pixels over.

✓ SELECTION TIP: INVERTING SELECTIONS

Sometimes it helps to select what you don't want in a picture. For instance, if the background is one colour it can be easier to select it and then invert the selection (**Select>Inverse**) to isolate the foreground subject. The Magic Wand Tool is ideal for this type of selection, as, with one click, you can select a white background. Below, we used a mask to show you the areas that are not selected.

✓ **Background selected**

✓ **Selection inversed**

Secrets unlocked

✓ SAVE SELECTION

If you spend some time preparing a selection, you might want to save it in case you want to use it again later. To do this, go to **Select>Save Selection**, give it a name in the dialogue box and click **OK**. The selection will be saved as a new channel, which can be accessed via **Window>Channel**. To load a saved selection, choose **Load Selection** from the Select menu or click the **Load Channel as a Selection** button at the bottom of the Channels palette.

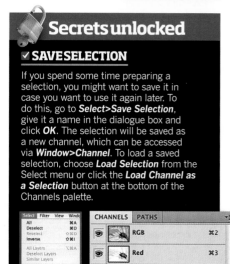

Quick Selection Tool

PC & MAC QUICK SELECT KEY
FOR PHOTOSHOP CS & ELEMENTS =

Learn how to make fast and accurate colour-based selections using one of the smartest selection tools in Photoshop's extensive arsenal

INTRODUCED IN CS3, the Quick Selection Tool is a cross between a brush and the Magic Wand Tool, and actually learns as you use it. It's similar to the Magic Wand Tool in that it makes a selection based on colour, but you can also control the selection by the brush *Size* slider. Also, if you drag the tool over your subject and it selects too much, hold down *Alt* to subtract from the selection and when you come to add to your selection again, you'll find the tool has remembered the areas you want to avoid. Smart, huh? The more information you give it about the regions you want and the regions you don't want, the smarter it becomes about your selection.

❶ **Selection mode:** New selection; Add to selection; Subtract from selection.
❷ **Brush:** Adjust the brush Size and Hardness.
❸ **Sample All Layers:** Sample colours from a composite image that has multiple layers.
❹ **Auto Enhance:** Analyses the edges for a better selection. Always keep this ticked.
❺ **Refine Edge:** This becomes active once you've made an initial selection.

1 To change the colour of an object in your picture, set a medium brush (**143px**) and click on it once or twice in the centre of the object.

2 Next, click on **Refine Edge** and slightly adjust the **Radius**, **Smooth** and **Feather** sliders to make the selection's transition more gradual.

3 Next go to **Image> Adjustments> Replace Color** and drag the **Fuzziness** slider to **200**. Then select the **eyedropper** with the **+** sign and click on areas of the object that aren't white. Now adjust the **Hue** slider to change the colour.

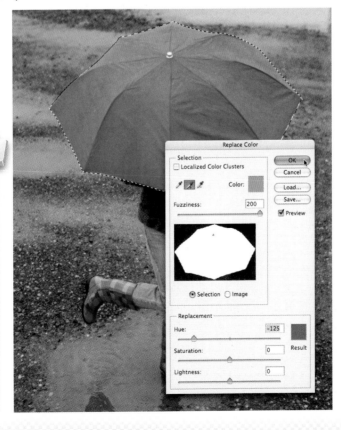

HOW DO I...

Change brushes?
As you need to 'paint' your selection in, brushes are integral to the Quick Selection Tool. For the best results, make your brush smaller the closer you get to the edges. Adjust the brush **Size** by clicking the brackets [and].

Software highlights

☑ CS5: SMART RADIUS

If you're selecting an object with areas that merge with the background, for instance strands of hair that you want to include, use the **Quick Selection Tool** to select only the main subject, avoiding these transitional areas and the background. Then access **Refine Edge**, one of the most advanced tools, and select **Smart Radius** and drag the **Radius** slider. You'll find the hair strands are picked out from the background without selecting the background, as it differentiates the edges.

☑ ELEMENTS 9: MAGIC EXTRACTOR

If you want to pluck a subject out from a background, Elements 9 has a nifty tool called Magic Extractor. It works like the Quick Selection Tool in that you only need to guide Elements and its intuitive functions will do the rest. Go to **Image>Magic Extractor**. Click on the **Foreground Brush** and roughly draw within the area of the image you want to keep, then switch to the **Background Brush** and add marks to the area you want to get rid of. Add a **Feather** and defringe, then click **OK**.

Secrets unlocked

☑ PIXEL MASKS

To make non-destructive adjustments to your selection, you can convert your selection into a mask, which means any changes you make to the colour, contrast and refinement of the selection do not affect the original image pixels. You can also revert to your selection at any time to edit your adjustments. To do this, create your selection and then click **Window>Masks** to bring up the Masks panel. Click on the **Add Pixel Mask** button at the top. Now you can add a Feather, access Refine Edge via the Mask Edge button, Color Range, Invert and copy the selection to another image, all without affecting the original pixels.

UP TO £100

focus on forever

GITZO SCRAPPAGE SCHEME

5 STAR
★★★★★
DEALER

AVAILABLE EXCLUSIVELY AT GITZO
5 STAR DEALER STOCKISTS. AS EASY AS 1, 2, 3...

STEP ONE
Trade in your old tripod, monopod or head
(or combination of) directly through Gitzo

STEP TWO
Make a like-for-like tripod, monopod
or head purchase (or combination of)

STEP THREE
Send in your old camera support and proof of purchase
to Gitzo in order to receive your Scrappage Allowance

Gitzo Scrappage Scheme promotion runs between 20th February – 31st August 2012

Gitzo™
A Vitec Group brand

For more information: T +44 01293 583300   F +44 01293 583301
E info@manfrottodistribution.co.uk   W www.gitzo.co.uk/scrappage

Improving a selection with Refine Edge

It's relatively easy to loosely select an area in an image that you wish to remove, move or manipulate. Where many photographers struggle is refining their selection to make transitions seamless. Here's how…

REFINE EDGE is one of the most advanced features in the selection arsenal as it allows you to fine-tune and control your selection for a seamless finish, regardless of what tool you use to make the selection. You can access the same features bundled in the Refine Edge function individually by clicking **Select>Modify**, but it doesn't give you the advantage of previewing your changes like Refine Edge does.

■ **Radius:** Use this to soften the edges of the selection, to improve the smoothness of the transition between the selection and background, and to target soft edges such as fur.

■ **Contrast:** Use the slider to make the edges sharper and to remove artifacts.

■ **Smooth:** Soften the edges without rounding the corners, then use **Radius** to restore some of the detail afterwards.

■ **Feather:** For more dramatic smoothing and blending with the surrounding area, it's an integral part of the selection process. How much feather you add depends on the resolution of your file and how soft an edge you want.

■ **Contract/Expand:** Shrink or enlarge the selection until it fits the subject perfectly.

■ **Preview options:** As a default, you can view your selection on a white background, but you can also view it on black or as a Layer Mask, for instance.

For the best results, use **Contract/Expand** and **Radius** to adjust the selection, followed by **Feather** and **Contrast** to refine the edges.

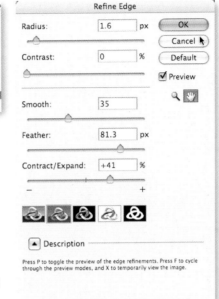

☑ REFINE EDGE IN CS5: Adobe should be given a round of applause for the upgrade they've given to this function. Refine Edge has acquired more control and intelligence. While using Channels in CS4 is really the only way you can get a clean selection of a subject with fine details around the edges, you can now select Smart Radius, which differentiates between hard and soft edges for more precise, detailed selections. Other new features include Shift Edge: an improved version of Contract/Expand and Output, which is really where this function shines. Under the drop-down menu Output To, you can opt for your selection to be converted into a Layer Mask or New Layer so you're not affecting the original image pixels.

Secrets unlocked

☑ COLOR RANGE

Accessible via the Select menu, the Color Range command is one of the quickest ways to select areas of specific colour or tone. It's also the only place you can alter the colour of the highlights, mid-tones and shadows independently as well as any other colours out of gamut. To make a selection, go to **Select>Color Range** and from the drop-down menu titled **Select**, pick the colour or tone you want to target. You'll see the related area highlighted in the preview window. You can also use the eyedropper to sample a colour that you want to select. To target one area of an image, like a person, draw a loose selection around it before accessing the Color Range command.

Secrets unlocked

☑ QUICK MASK MODE

You can preview your selection and edit it using Quick Mask Mode, which is represented as a semi-transparent coloured overlay. You can apply this mask by either clicking on the **Edit in Quick Mask Mode** button at the bottom of the toolbar or clicking **Select>Edit in Quick Mask Mode**. You can also use the keyboard shortcut **Q** to switch back and forth between the selection and Quick Mask Mode. To edit the selection in Quick Mask Mode, use the **Brush Tool** to expand or fill in the selection. Set the **Foreground color** to **White** to erase the mask and expand the selection and the **Foreground color** to **Black** to subtract from the selection.

RAW

Learning to edit Raw files could be the key to fantastic results. In this section we reveal
how it can help improve the quality and flexibility of your Photoshop editing

AS ALL EXPERIENCED photographers are aware, the very best images are a combination of great in-camera technique followed by top Photoshop skills. And, arguably, the most essential step starts by shooting in Raw format, rather than JPEG, to capture the most amount of information. To use a film analogy, the Raw file is like a negative that you can interpret in the darkroom how you wish. By letting the camera do the developing to produce a JPEG image, you've effectively let the camera produce the print while you've thrown away the negative!

There's no such thing as a .RAW file in the same way that there's .JPEG and .TIFF. Instead, Raw is a catch-all term used to describe the data captured directly from a camera's sensor, which comes in a variety of flavours, depending on the brand of camera. Examples include .CR2 for Canon and .NEF for Nikon. Data in this form is greyscale and not a lot of use to the camera user on its own.

There are two methods of converting Raw files into usable image data. The first happens automatically in-camera whenever you select the JPEG setting. The second method is to shoot in Raw mode and convert your Raw files post-capture using a PC or Mac and a Raw converter such as Adobe Camera Raw. The latter is the best option for maximum quality as it provides access to the full 16-bit range of information, giving you more room to make adjustments and correct problems like under- and overexposure.

While there are many advantages to Raw files, the main one being that editing is non-destructive, the principle disadvantage of shooting Raw is the extra time involved. JPEGs are ready to roll straight out of camera. Raw files on the other hand require the extra step of opening in Camera Raw, making the necessary changes and then processing. It's not difficult, though, read on to find out how to do it.

The toolbar

At the top-left corner of the interface are various symbols, each with a use to edit your pictures. CS5 has a few new additions to the CS4 arsenal, which we outline below, but the main tools you'll use for everyday Raw editing are the Zoom, Hand, Rotate and White Balance tools. Others, such as Color Sampler, Crop, Straighten and Retouch tools, work well, but unless you're editing solely in Raw, are best left to Photoshop once the Raw file is processed. Red-eye removal is handy if you need it, but you're unlikely to process many portraits shot in Raw that suffer from red-eye!

1) Zoom Tool: Magnify the image to see it in more detail.

2) Hand Tool: Navigate around the magnified image.

3) White Balance Tool: Allows you to correct and set a custom White Balance by clicking on neutral areas in the preview image, such as white.

4) Color Sampler Tool: Allows you to select a colour to adjust by clicking on that area of the image.

5) Crop Tool: Use to crop images.

6) Straighten Tool: Correct a wonky horizon or rotate.

7) Retouch Tool: Gets rid of sensor spots and other unwanted blemishes.

8) Red-Eye Removal Tool: Click on the eye to remove red-eye.

9) Preferences: Click here to access the Camera Raw Preferences dialogue box

10) Rotate counterclockwise & Rotate clockwise tools: Rotate anti-clockwise or clockwise by 90°.

11) Targeted Adjustment Tool: Instead of using the sliders, drag this tool on the image to make edits (CS5).

12) Adjustment Brush: Use this tool to make localised edits to the image (CS5).

13) Graduated Filter: Draw a line across your image to recreate the effect of a Graduated Filter. You can then adjust the Exposure, Brightness, Contrast, Saturation, Clarity, Sharpness and Color of the filter to suit your picture (CS5).

Open object

Once you've done all your necessary Raw editing, press **Shift** to turn the **Open** button to **Open Object** to process your Raw file in Photoshop as a Smart Object. The benefit of a Smart Object is that you can double-click on the layer in Photoshop to reopen the Raw file and continue any Raw edits in ACR. Alternatively, hold down **Alt** to turn the **Open** button to **Open Copy** (so you don't work on the original Raw file in Photoshop) and the **Cancel** button to **Reset** to revert your image back to its original state.

Understand your Raw converter

To go from an original Raw file to a final image, 'process' it using a Raw converter like Adobe Camera Raw

Any technical process seems complicated and daunting when you try it for the first time. Remember taking your first digital photograph or 'Photoshopping' your first image? Chances are you didn't have a clue what you were doing, but through trial and error and making lots of mistakes, you got there in the end. It's the same with processing your Raw files in software like Adobe Camera Raw.

The main reason why photographers stick to shooting in JPEG is because it's quick, easy and safe: the camera does the complicated stuff and all you're left with are a few tweaks in Photoshop or Lightroom to finish the job off.

Shooting in Raw, on the other hand, involves another steep learning curve because every shot you take needs to be worked on. It's the digital equivalent to going from taking your films to a high street lab for processing and printing, to setting up a darkroom and doing the job yourself. Do you think it's really worth all the hassle?

In a word, yes! To realise your full potential as a photographer, you need to take control of your photography and the only way to really do this is to shoot and process Raw files. Over the next few pages, we'll give you a rundown of the main controls and tools available in Photoshop's Raw converter – Adobe Camera Raw – with an explanation of what they do and how to use them, starting with the Basics tab which features everything you need for a simple conversion.

The basic tools for Raw conversion

Most of Adobe's Raw controls are adjusted via sliders, making them fast and easy to use. Here are the key features located under the Basics tab:

⊘ **Adjustment panels:** The main controls you're going to use when processing Raw files are to be found on the right side of the Raw Interface, between the histogram and the control sliders. There are eight icons covering the following set of options (from left to right): Basic, Tone Curve, Detail, HSL/Grayscale, Split Toning, Lens Corrections, Camera Calibrations and Presets.

⊘ **Vibrance and Saturation:** This tool is an alternative to the Saturation slider, which adjusts all the colours in an image equally. The Vibrance Tool, on the other hand, affects colours that need boosting, having less effect on the colours already high in saturation.

⊘ **Blacks:** This slider shifts the left part of the histogram even more to the left, making the blacks in the image a lot more dominant, and is a useful way of increasing the overall contrast.

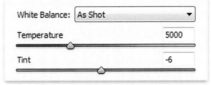

⊘ **White Balance:** Shooting in Raw means that you can control the White Balance in post-production, rather than having to select the right White Balance preset in-camera. Under the Basic tab, you have all the in-camera WB presets available in a drop-down menu to pick from (eg Auto, Daylight, Cloudy etc). You can also use the Temperature and Tint sliders to create your own Custom WB. Alternatively, you could use the White Balance Tool, found in the toolbar.

⊘ **Fill Light:** Fill Light attempts to recover details from shadows, without brightening any blacks. Similar to using fill-in flash, this tool will cast some light into your foreground. Use it with the Blacks slider to add more punch, but be careful not to overdo it for unnatural results.

⊘ **Clarity:** Adds depth to an image by increasing local contrast, with the greatest effect on the mid-tones. It works similar to a large radius Unsharp Mask in Photoshop. Zoom into the image 100% to see the effects and stop when you start to see halos appear near the edges in the image.

⊘ **Exposure:** Found at the top of the Basics tab, under White Balance, the Exposure slider adjusts the overall brightness of the image, with greater focus on the highlights. The values are in increments equivalent to f/stops. For many photographers, this tool is their saving grace as it allows them to correct their in-camera exposure. Watch out for noise and artefacts creeping in when you push the exposure too far. Use in conjunction with Recovery to reduce the highlight values.

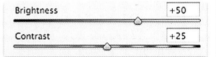

⊘ **Brightness/Contrast:** Brightness works in a similar way to Exposure. However, instead of clipping the highlights and shadows, it compresses and expands the information. Set the overall tonal range first using the Exposure, Recover and Blacks sliders, then adjust Brightness. The Contrast slider mainly affects mid-tones, causing them to brighten or darken to increase contrast.

⊘ **Recovery:** This is an image saver for anyone who has slightly overexposed their highlights. This nifty tool should obviously not be relied upon, but is definitely one of the most invaluable features in ACR as it can recover mid-tone detail from clipped highlights. It's not a miracle worker, though: the detail has to be there to begin with.

Raw interface

When you open a Raw file in Adobe Camera Raw, you're presented with this interface. The preview image shows the Raw image in its original state.

14) Zoom: You can vary the size of the preview image and also zoom into it using the tabs in the bottom left-hand corner of the interface.

15) Workflow Option: At the bottom of the screen is the Workflow Option. If you click on this, a dialogue box opens, giving you various options. For *Space* (colour space), *Adobe RGB (1998)* is most widely used. For *Depth*, choose *16 Bits/Channel*. For *Size*, go for the one that matches the pixel resolution of your camera (no point paying for those megapixels then not using them!). And for *Resolution*, enter *300 pixels/inch*.

16) Histogram: In the top right-hand corner is the image's histogram, which shows the distribution of tones in the Red, Green and Blue channels. Where you see Cyan, it indicates a crossover between the green and blue channels, Yellow is the crossover between red and green channels, and Magenta is the crossover between red and blue channels. White shows where all three channels crossover. Use the histogram to judge the exposure as you adjust the sliders.

17) Clipping warning: The two triangular tabs in the top left and right of the histogram tell you if there has been any clipping of the highlights or shadows. If the triangles are black, no clipping has occurred. If the tabs change colour, the colour tells you that a colour channel or a combination of channels have been clipped. If the triangle is white, all three channels are clipped. If you click on the tabs, areas in the preview images will be highlighted to show where clipping has occurred – clipped shadows show as flashing blue and clipped highlights as flashing red.

Basics of batch processing

The curse and cure of digital is being able to shoot lots of images at no additional cost, but what's the best way to manage all the files?

Caroline Wilkinson: You've got files upon files of Raw images and you're not sure what to do with them or how to sort them out. The beauty of Raw is that you may have a hidden gem among pictures that appear to have little potential, due to the wide parameters that software, like Adobe Camera Raw, gives you for retrieving detail and correcting exposure. Before you can assess how usable your shots

are, you need to do a few adjustments to eek out the weak from the strong and the salvageable from print-ready. Thankfully, you can do this quickly in Adobe Camera Raw by batch-processing images. Most of these steps can be expanded upon – for instance, White Balance, exposure and colour – depending on how much work your images need, but when it comes to getting images ready as quickly as possible, follow this step-by-step guide.

1 Load up your images Organise your files into batches, divided by what lighting conditions they were shot in/White Balance used. In Photoshop CS, go to **File>Open** and then select a batch of images by holding **Shift** and clicking the first and last image. Click **Open** to transfer into ACR. Flick through the images on the big screen and select **backspace** to reject any that are out of focus; a red cross will appear in the corner of the image and it won't be affected by any other edits.

2 Correct lens distortion This step is much easier if all your images have been shot with the same lens. If they've not, you'll have to adjust each image individually. Click **Select All** at the top of the thumbnail palette and then select the **Lens Corrections** tab and tick **Enable Lens Profile Corrections**. If the details under Lens Profile are incorrect or the vignetting needs further adjustments, use the sliders under the **Manual** tab. Under Manual, select **Defringe: All Edges**.

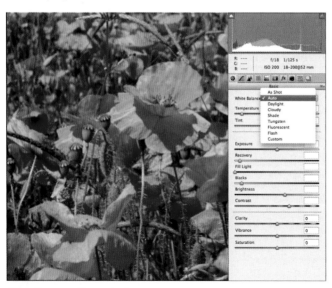

3 Adjust tonality and colour With all the images still selected, click on to the **Basic** tab and press **Auto** (just above Exposure) to correct the images' tonality. Next, click on the **White Balance** drop-down menu and select your correct WB setting – I picked Auto. While this is the quickest way to batch-process a large amount of images take in the same lighting, you can always return to these settings later to refine the tonality and even pick a different WB preset for creative effect.

4 Selective White Balance Being able to correct colour casts with a click of a button is one of the biggest assets of working with Raw images. Note that you can also set a custom WB using the White Balance Tool in the toolbar. Click on a white area of the image to set the correct WB (even better, take a shot of a white sheet of paper as part of your batch of images and click on this to set the WB for the rest of the batch). Try clicking on a different area of the image to see what colour effects you can achieve, too.

Final image
Making adjustments to batches is far simpler and less laborious than if you were to correct images one by one – and your standout shot will become obvious.

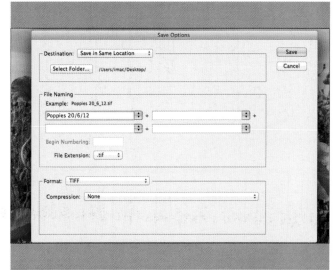

5 Straighten and crop At this stage, I recommend flicking through the images once again and rejecting any images you're sure you don't want by pressing the *backspace* key. It's now time to address the images individually. If an image needs to be realigned, select the *Straighten Tool* from the toolbar and click and drag it along the horizon and release. Then press *Enter* to confirm the crop. You can use the *Crop Tool*, too, if you need to refine the composition of any of your images.

6 Save images At this stage, you can either work on the images that need more attention in ACR, open in Photoshop by clicking *Select All* and *Open*, or if this blitz of basic adjustments was enough, you can save the files. To do this, click *Select All* then *Save Images*… In the dialogue box, select the folder you want to save the images to and then give the batch a name, eg 'Poppies 20/6/12'. To keep the maximum amount of data for editing in Photoshop, select *TIFF* as a *Format* and *Compression: None*.

Recovering your exposure

It's rarely too late to give your ill-exposed Raw shots some TLC –
here's how to take those images from bland to beautiful…

Original Raw

Caroline Wilkinson: Part of the pleasure of shooting in Raw format is its flexibility and forgiveness. If you mess up the exposure, ACR is there to help and maybe even salvage an image from the scrap heap: it's a photographer's safety net. Even though I'd never imagine that our readers wouldn't try to get a shot right in-camera, accidents do happen: you forget to alter settings between shots, you don't have the right ND grad filters to hand or maybe your camera's playing up (we find it's always best to blame your gear for an ill-exposed image) – but now there are no excuses really. As long as you don't overexpose an image too much, 'blowing out' detail in the highlights to the point that it's irretrievable, ACR can save your image. In fact, by exposing to the right slightly (overexposing by a stop or two) and using Raw conversion software, you can end up with an image containing far more detail as it's the brightest end of the tonal range that contains the most information. The best way to keep on top of this is to turn on your highlight warning facility on your camera's histogram, so if you have overexposed an image too much, these areas should flash red on the LCD screen. You can also check via Adobe Camera Raw. Here's how…

1 Open your file When you first open your image in ACR, study the histogram. Assess what types of adjustments need to be made. In this image, you can see that the colours and tones are quite light, with the histogram weighted to the right, so it's likely that some detail in the highlights needs to be recovered and the Exposure slider reduced a stop or two to reveal detail.

2 Recover highlights Click on the warning symbol (yellow triangle in top right) to see where and how many highlights have been clipped, identifiable by the areas flashing red. Move the *Recovery* slider to retrieve as much detail as possible in the highlight regions, but be aware that this slider reduces image contrast so don't overuse it at the expense of the rest of the image.

3 Exposure adjustment You may find that adjusting the *Exposure* slider by a stop or two can help correct most exposure errors. But if you've underexposed your image, be aware that if you add too much exposure you'll reveal noise hidden in the shadows. Try balancing the *Exposure* slider with the *Fill Light* slider to reveal detail in the darks and to brighten mid-tones.

4 Boost colour & contrast Combine *Fill Light* with *Blacks* to improve contrast (you can also use the *Contrast* slider – just be aware of clipping any highlights). Next, adjust the *Vibrance* to pump up the colour. Use the *White Balance Tool* or access White Balance *Presets* from the drop-down menu to correct any colour casts or to change the temperature for creative effect.

5 Make selective adjustments If there are areas of shadow or highlights that require more help to reveal detail, but you don't want to affect the image globally, use the *Adjustment Brush*. Located in the top toolbar, this feature is great for non-destructive dodging and burning. To target shadows, click *New* to create a new brush and then *Show Mask.* Brush over the area you want to affect, using the mask as a guide.

6 Repeat the process Once you're happy, click on *Show Mask* again to see your edits and use the various sliders to adjust the look of that area, such as *Sharpness*, *Exposure* and *Contrast*. You can then use the same brush to apply these adjustments to other areas of the image. Use the *Size* and *Feather* sliders to change the features of the brush. To create a new adjustment, say for the highlights, click *New* and repeat the process.

7 Edit your adjustments You can add as many new adjustment brushes as you need to target any size area of your image. To re-edit an adjustment, click on the corresponding pin on your image and adjust the sliders. To remove an adjustment, click *Erase* and brush over that particular area. Once happy, save as a *TIFF* to edit in Photoshop if needed. Click *Done* to keep the edited file or *Cancel* to keep it in its original state.

Final image
Revealing the lost detail and colour from an overexposed shot adds plenty of warmth and vibrance.

Combining Raw files

Get the perfect image by merging two shots for ultimate quality

Luke Marsh: Setting your camera to shoot in Raw means you're able to recover hidden detail from areas of a scene that are over- or underexposed. The Raw converter in Photoshop Elements, used here, works in much the same way as CS. You need to create two separate images of different exposures from the same Raw file – one for the sky and the other for the foreground– then combine them for the perfect result. Not only will we show how to adjust exposure post-capture, you'll also find out how to use the High Pass filter for sharpening and how to make colour adjustments. This technique is especially efficient as you are only working with image data captured in a single exposure, so you can revisit any of your old Raw files to try it.

Raw file

1 Open the file When you open a Raw file in Elements the image appears in the Raw control window (above). As the foreground in the original Raw file is well exposed, little work is needed at this stage on the image. Simply click *Open*, leaving the settings as they are, then go to *File>Save As* and create a Photoshop file (.PSD) as we are going to be working with layers.

2 Repeat Reopen the original Raw file, and again the Raw control window appears with the image. This time use the *Exposure* control (circled) and move the slider left to underexpose the image, pulling back the hidden detail from the original Raw file's overexposed sky. When you're happy with the results, click *Open* to take the image into Elements.

3 Copy & paste You now have two files open. One contains the original exposure and the other is the new underexposed image. With the underexposed file active, click *Select>All* then *Edit>Copy*, placing the image into the pasteboard memory. Now you can close this file and use *Edit>Paste* to place this image into a new layer on the original file.

4 Remove foreground With the two exposures in place, we now want to combine the correctly exposed foreground with the newly exposed sky. With the sky layer active and using the *Rectangular Marquee Tool*, select a large area of foreground, just short of the horizon. Next, click *Edit>Delete* to remove the area, noting the effect in the Layers palette preview (inset).

5 Clean up Now it's time to tidy up the horizon, so with the *Eraser Tool* set to a medium-sized, soft-edged brush and the *Opacity* set to around **55%**, gradually erase areas of the newly exposed layer along the horizon, revealing the original foreground image. The slight feathering between the two layers creates a misty effect that enhances the image's mood.

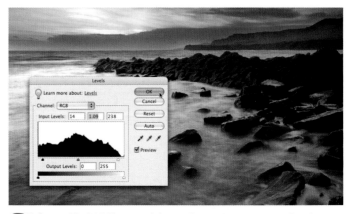

6 Enhance The initial layer work is complete, so to save your work so far, go to *Layer>Flatten Image* then *File>Save As* to create a new file. With both layers merged, it's time for some overall enhancement, so click on *Enhance>Adjust Lighting>Levels* to lighten up the image and improve the definition. Click *OK* to apply the changes.

Final image
Stormy skies overhead! It's clear to see the benefits of shooting your images in Raw, as it's possible to rescue more detail than if you'd captured the scene as a JPEG.

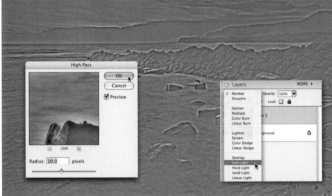

7 High Pass The High Pass filter is a far more forgiving way to enhance detail than sharpening. To use it, first go to *Layer>Duplicate Layer* to preserve the original image. Then go to *Filter>Other>High Pass*, adjusting the *Radius* to around *20* pixels before clicking *OK*. Now you need to change the *Blend Mode* in the Layers palette to *Soft Light*.

8 Darken areas Use *Layer>Flatten Image* again, saving a copy if required. Now, using the *Burn Tool* (inset) with a large soft-edged brush and the *Opacity* set to approximately *25%*, darken the exposure of specific areas, which helps to improve the depth of the image. Focus on the edges of the frame and gradually build the effect up.

9 Select sky The image is predominantly blue in hue and we'd quite like to inject a different tone to the sky area. Using the *Rectangular Marquee Tool*, select the area above the horizon and *Select>Feather*, entering an amount of *50* pixels to soften the selection, before clicking *Edit>Copy* then *Edit>Paste*, placing the selection into a new layer.

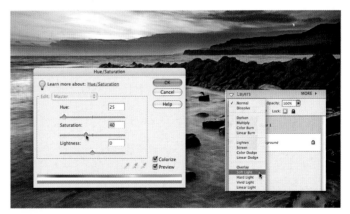

10 Adjust colour Change the *Blend Mode* of the new layer to *Soft Light*, and then go to *Enhance>Adjust Colour>Adjust Hue/Saturation*. In the window, start by clicking the *Colorize* box and immediately see the effect in the preview. Finally, adjust the *Hue* and *Saturation* sliders until you are happy with the colour, and then click *OK*.

I AM MARCO POLO

I AM THE NIKON D7000. I am outstanding image quality and impressive performance, together with the range of NIKKOR lenses, I am ready to fulfill your passion. With 16.2 megapixels CMOS image sensor and 2,016-pixel RGB metering sensor, an EXPEED 2 processor, a 39-point AF system and full HD movie recording. I am a new era of creativity. **www.nikon.co.uk**

At the heart of the image **Nikon**

Step-by-step tutorials

BASIC TECHNIQUES

Our favourite Photoshop skills help you make a major difference with minimum effort

Be dramatic with your black & white conversions

Monochrome images can have incredible impact – here's how to get the look right…

Caroline Wilkinson: When shooting landscapes, most of us give little thought to how scenes may appear in black & white. This is understandable, as for most of us, the shots we take remain mainly in colour. Now we're not suggesting that in future you imagine how every scene you shoot will look in mono, but we would suggest you consider it from time to time. Shooting images to convert to black & white is somewhat of a discipline and when you capture a scene with the intention of making it monochrome, a few factors may affect the impact of your picture. To stop an image appearing lifeless without colour, you need to pay particular attention to the composition, tonal range, shapes and foreground interest.

First of all, it's worth avoiding areas with highly saturated colour, like sunsets and fields of bluebells, poppies and canola, as a black & white image simply won't do them justice. Remember that every colour has its own shade of grey when converted to mono, so you're looking for scenes that show a range of lights and darks, otherwise the image can look flat and lack tonal range. Form is a vital ingredient of mono landscapes, so look for scenes with textures, strong lines and bold shapes that help create contrast, and foreground interest that leads the eye in to the scene. Rough weather can add drama; stormy skies are wonderful. You should avoid cloudless skies, as these give grey, lifeless results. If clouds are more wispy than substantial, you can use the Burn Tool to selectively adjust their exposure, darkening them to add drama.

While directional light provides good contrast, we can't always rely on the perfect photo conditions. For this reason, we'll show you how you can selectively adjust exposure using the Dodge and Burn tools to transform your mellow mid-tones into highlights and shadows for extra impact.

Converting your image to mono in Adobe Camera Raw or using a Black & White adjustment layer can give great results, but we shouldn't neglect the Channel Mixer, which was a favourite method for many until CS3. It's a step up in quality and a lot more controllable than a Grayscale conversion. And while not as advanced as the other methods, it is one of the best ways to get extreme contrast.

1 Make Raw adjustments Open your image in Adobe Camera Raw. The first thing that you should do is make any necessary exposure adjustments to get the image how you want it to look. For this image, we adjusted the Exposure slider by adding a positive value to lighten the picture and the Blacks slider to slightly increase contrast.

2 Prepare for Photoshop When you come to open the image in Photoshop, hold down *Shift* to change the Open Image button into Open Object. This way, if you want to edit the Raw files again later – say you want to adjust the exposure further – you can double-click on the Object layer in Photoshop to revert back to Adobe Camera Raw.

3 Add an Adjustment Layer Now duplicate the layer (*Layer> Duplicate Layer*) and rasterise the image so that you can edit it by clicking on the image. Click *OK*. Next go to *Layer>New Adjustment Layer>Channel Mixer* to open its dialogue box. Using an Adjustment Layer means if you want to undo your conversion, you can just delete the layer as you haven't affected the original image.

4 Convert to mono Click on the *Monochrome* box in the Channel Mixer dialogue box to turn the image black & white. Now use the sliders to adjust the *Red*, *Green* and *Blue* channels to improve the contrast. For the best results, avoid clipping any highlights or shadows by making sure the total value of the sliders amount to *100%*. You can check the amount under the sliders.

5 How NOT to do it The total value here is 200% – while the shadows are well exposed, the highlights have been clipped and we've lost detail in the sky and the water. It's all about finding the right balance. If you find you have a couple of hotspots or dark areas that you can't get right using the Channel Mixer, you'll be able to correct these in the next step – just try to avoid doing it in excess.

Final image
By using the Dodge and Burn tools you can bring over and underexposed areas back from the brink for a brilliant mono result.

6 Selectively lighten Click back to the Layers palette and select the duplicate layer. If you have some areas that need lightening, select the *Dodge Tool* from the toolbar and select a large, soft brush from the Options bar. We used a diameter of 900px and 0% Hardness. Also from the Option bar, select *Shadows* from the *Range* drop-down menu, set the *Exposure* as low as **4%** and check *Protect Tones* to minimise artefacts.

7 Continue editing Brush over the area you want to lighten. If your brush is too hard or your Exposure is too high, you'll find you'll make circles over the areas you work on. For the best results, you want to build the effect up softly. Zooming in to the area by holding *Cmd* and **+** can help. Now switch the *Range* to *Midtone* and, adjusting the brush *Size* and *Exposure* as necessary, work on lightening the grey areas.

8 Repeat Using the *Burn Tool*, found underneath the *Dodge Tool*, repeat step seven. Set a low *Exposure*, select a soft, large brush and the *Range* to *Midtone*. Focus on the shadow areas and the darker mid-tones, increasing contrast by getting rid of as much grey as possible, without losing any detail, and boosting the blacks. If done right, this step can make the clouds look particularly dramatic.

Create a toned mono image

Apply coloured tones to your black & white shots to great effect…

Luke Marsh: There is so much you can do with a black & white photograph. You can play with its tones and contrast, make local dodge and burn adjustments to parts of the scene and even apply coloured tones or tints to give a certain look and feel. This last part is easy to do badly, but looks great when it's done well. A slightly warm, brown cast (known as 'sepia') is reminiscent of those old photographs of yesteryear and gives the picture a classic look. Alternatively, a cooler blue tone gives pictures a more modern, contemporary look. The secret is to experiment and not go over the top, and start off with a good monochrome conversion. Here's how to really take control of your image and make the best job of it.

Original

1 Open your image With the image open, add a *Black & White* adjustment layer by clicking the *Create new fill or adjustment layer* icon at the bottom of the Layers palette. In CS3 or earlier versions of the software, you can use a *Channel Mixer* adjustment layer instead.

2 Tweak the tones Adjust the colour sliders until your image contains a pleasing array of tones or choose a preset from the drop-down menu. If working with the Channel Mixer, check *Monochrome* and alter the sliders, ensuring they all add up to *100*.

3 Boost the contrast Add a *Brightness/ Contrast* adjustment layer, uncheck the *Use Legacy* box and increase the *Contrast* to suit. With the *Layer Mask* thumbnail selected, use the *Brush Tool* and *Black* paint to hide areas of the adjustment.

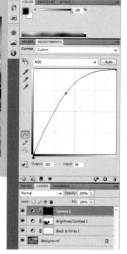

4 Make a Curves adjustment Add a *Curves* adjustment layer and push the curve hard upwards with a single point from the centre. Select its *Layer Mask* thumbnail and invert by pressing *Ctrl+I* to turn it from White to Black, hiding the effect.

5 Repeat step Add another *Curves* adjustment layer, only this time push the curves downwards with a single point from the centre. Invert the mask again. Now select a large brush with the *Hardness* set to *0%*, the *Opacity* at *10%* and *White* colour loaded.

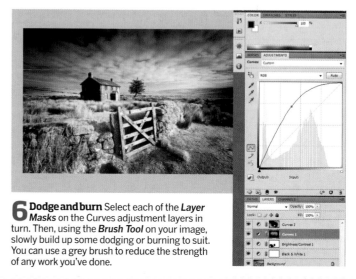

6 Dodge and burn Select each of the *Layer Masks* on the Curves adjustment layers in turn. Then, using the *Brush Tool* on your image, slowly build up some dodging or burning to suit. You can use a grey brush to reduce the strength of any work you've done.

Final image
The final step is to merge all the layers (*Layers>Merge Visible*) and to make any final colour adjustments.

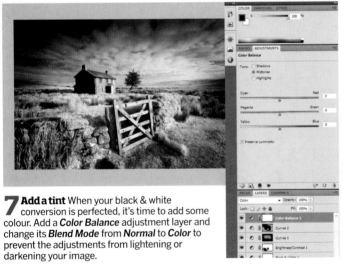

7 Add a tint When your black & white conversion is perfected, it's time to add some colour. Add a *Color Balance* adjustment layer and change its *Blend Mode* from *Normal* to *Color* to prevent the adjustments from lightening or darkening your image.

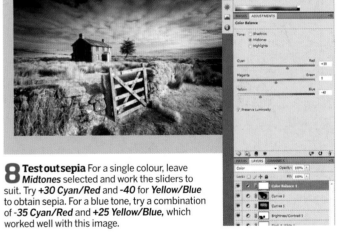

8 Test out sepia For a single colour, leave *Midtones* selected and work the sliders to suit. Try *+30 Cyan/Red* and *-40* for *Yellow/Blue* to obtain sepia. For a blue tone, try a combination of *-35 Cyan/Red* and *+25 Yellow/Blue,* which worked well with this image.

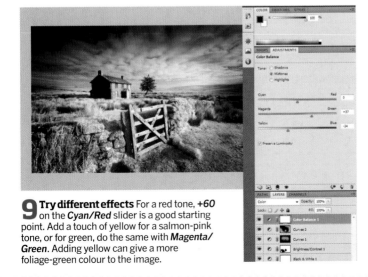

9 Try different effects For a red tone, *+60* on the *Cyan/Red* slider is a good starting point. Add a touch of yellow for a salmon-pink tone, or for green, do the same with *Magenta/ Green*. Adding yellow can give a more foliage-green colour to the image.

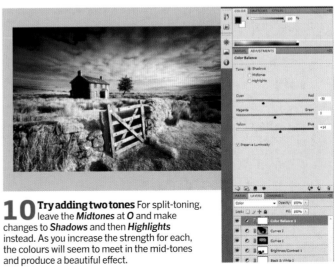

10 Try adding two tones For split-toning, leave the *Midtones* at *0* and make changes to *Shadows* and then *Highlights* instead. As you increase the strength for each, the colours will seem to meet in the mid-tones and produce a beautiful effect.

Basic skills for duotones

Add colour to highlights and shadows for fantastic effects with ease

Luke Marsh: Split-toning, or duotoning, dates back to the days of the chemical darkroom, but with digital processing, separately toning shadows and highlights has become much quicker and easier on the wallet. The treatment suits images with good tonal range, when there's clear distinction between the shadows and highlights, so that the colours don't overlap. There are so many colour combinations you can try: red and yellow work well, as do green and blue, but the effect can also be changed depending on which colour you use for highlights and which you use for shadows. For instance, red highlights and blue shadows give a contemporary, energising look, while red shadows and blue highlights can be unsettling. There are no hard and fast rules, though – mix it up until you hit on something you like.

1 Convert to monochrome
Elements users: duplicate the Background Layer with *Ctrl/Cmd+J* and run *Enhance> Convert to Black & White*. Photoshop users: add a Black & White adjustment layer using the *Create new Adjustment* icon in the Layers palette or by clicking *Layer>New Adjustment Layer*.

2 Adjust contrast
In both Elements and Photoshop, you have the option to choose a preset (use the drop-down menu in Photoshop) or work with the colour sliders to produce your desired contrast. Experiment freely with each method until you reach a look that suits the particular image in hand.

3 Apply colour Once the image is converted to black & white, in Photoshop, add a *Hue/ Saturation* adjustment layer and check the box that says *Colorize*. Before you go any further, change the layer's *Blend Mode* to *Color* using the drop-down menu at the top of the Layers palette to prevent the image being lightened or darkened.

4 Tone shadows Drag the *Hue* slider to pick the colour wash for the shadows. Ignore the fact that the colour is applied to the whole tonal range for now. Select the *Hue/Saturation* layer and select *Layer>Layer Style>Blending Options*. Hold *Alt* and click the white triangle on the *This Layer* slider to split it into two parts.

5 Adjust the colour Now drag the left-hand part of the triangle along to the *100* setting and the right-hand part to *175*. If you now click the *Preview* box on and off you can see how the highlight tones have been excluded from the toning. Click *OK* then add another *Hue/Saturation* adjustment layer, checking the *Colorize* box again.

6 Tone the highlights Change the layer's *Blend Mode* from Normal to *Color* and move the *Hue* slider to choose your highlight colour. Click *Layer>Layer Style>Blending Options* and split the black triangle. Set the right side to *155* and the left to *80*. Click *OK* to finish in Photoshop.

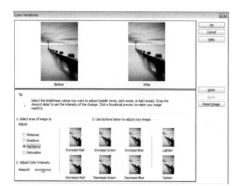

7 Use Variations Elements users don't have blending options so you need to use Variations (*Enhance>Adjust Color>Color Variations*). Now select *Shadows* on the left to start and click the relevant picture button to add the colour of your choice to the shadows.

8 Finishing touch Click as many times as you need to get the desired strength, and don't be afraid to mix colour tones. Use the subtract picture button if you go too far. Check the *Highlight* button when you're done and repeat for the highlight tones. Click *OK* to finish.

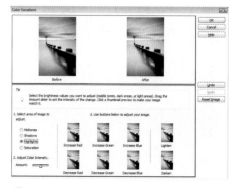

Final image

As you can see, the Photoshop treatment has given the former black & white image a new and appealing atmosphere.

Breathe life into flat photos

Want to create an HDR effect but don't have Raw files or a set of bracketed exposures? Don't despair! Use Shadows & Highlights…

Luke Marsh: We all have images that didn't quite render the scene how you remember it. Maybe the sky's not as moody, or the ground is too dark, or maybe the overall appearance of the image lacks contrast or is badly exposed. Well, Shadows & Highlights can resurrect these images. This nifty adjustment is a fantastic photographic tool, which is often overlooked by users since dedicated HDR software like Photomatix and Photoshop actions became available from third-party companies. In the simplest terms, the adjustments allow you to recover detail from over- or underexposed areas by adjusting the Highlights or Shadows controls respectively, or you can improve the overall tonal range using the Midtone Contrast slider. It's really very simple.

The key to success with Shadows & Highlights is subtlety. As with any process that plays with tonal range, HDR included, Shadows & Highlights can produce photographic Frankensteins if used too eagerly. So why not give it a go? The controls may seem daunting at first, but after a little experimentation and with a better understanding of what can be achieved, you may find you'll be using this feature regularly.

HOT KEY

Alt to reset
When working in Shadows & Highlights, hold down *Alt* to change the Cancel button to a Reset button in case you want to take the filter back to its default settings. You can also uncheck *Preview* to toggle between the blurred and original image.

Original

1 Duplicate original Our chosen image is a bit lifeless, yet clearly has potential texture in the sky and detail in the foreground that could be pulled out using Shadows & Highlights. First, create a duplicate layer from the original by going to *Layer>Duplicate Layer…*, naming the layer accordingly for reference later.

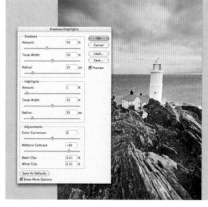

2 Shadows & Highlights On the duplicate layer go to *Image>Adjustments>Shadows & Highlights…* As the image is generally flat, concentrate on the *Shadows* and *Midtone Contrast*, with only minor adjustments to the *Highlight* field. At this stage you want to be focusing more on getting the foreground right.

3 Duplicate adjusted layer Now duplicate this edited layer with *Layer>Duplicate Layer…* Then add a Layer Mask by going to *Layer>Layer Mask>Reveal All* or by clicking on the *Add Layer Mask* icon at the bottom of the Layers palette (circled). The purpose of the Layer Mask is so that the next edit only affects the sky area of this layer.

4 Add a gradient Click on the *Layer Mask* thumbnail and select the *Gradient Tool*, ensuring the *Foreground* and *Background color* are set to the default *Black* and *White*. With the *Shift* key held down to ensure a straight line, click near the horizon and drag, letting go at the top of the image. This adds a gradient to the mask.

5 Create a stormy sky With the mask in place, any work done will only affect the sky area. Open *Shadows & Highlights* as instructed in step two, but this time work mainly on the *Highlights* and *Midtones Contrast* to pull all the detail back into the sky. You may want to increase the *Black Clip* to improve the overall contrast.

6 Reduce the saturation One final tweak is to remove some of the colour to enhance the storm-like appearance of the image. With the top layer still active, go to *Layer>New Adjustment Layer>Hue/Saturation…* and reduce the *Saturation* slider by around *20%*, then click *OK*. Now save as a *PSD*, to preserve all the layers.

Final image
From flat to fantastic: Shadows &
Highlights has pulled out lots of
detail that lay hidden in the JPEG.

Create an ND grad filter

If you're potentially great landscape images are spoilt by wishy-washy skies, learn how to improve them with a digital ND grad filter effect

Caroline Wilkinson: When faced with a landscape that has a bright sky and dark foreground, most digital photographers would reach for their Neutral Density graduate filters to even out the exposure and retain the detail in the sky. But if you're ever caught without an ND grad filter, there are certain steps you can take using Photoshop to recover detail in the sky later and avoid a flat, lifeless result. In the same way that an ND grad filter bleeds from grey at the top to clear at the bottom, underexposing the sky while keeping the exposure of the foreground the same, Photoshop's Gradient Tool can produce a near-identical effect digitally in both CS5 and Elements 10.

Original

HELEN DIXON

1 Open Raw image It's best to photograph a landscape in Raw format as you'll be able to recover more detail. First duplicate your image so you have two versions. You'll be processing one for detail in the sky and the other for the landscape.

2 Edit Raw files Open file one in Adobe Camera Raw and, focusing on the foreground, adjust the *Exposure* and *Recovery* slider to get the desired effect. If you make any other adjustments, make a note to replicate them in the sky image.

3 Repeat for the sky Once you've finished editing, click *Open Image*. Now open file two to edit the sky in ACR. You may need to be more dramatic with your adjustments here to recover lost highlights. When done, click *Open Image*.

4 Merge layers With both images open, use the *Move Tool* to click and drag the land image, holding down *Shift*, on top of the sky shot. Now you should be able to see the image with the correctly exposed foreground but not the sky.

5 Apply Gradient Map Go to *Image>New Adjustment Layer>Gradient Map*. Make sure it's set on *Foreground to Background*. Drag the new layer under the top image layer and link them by holding *Alt* and clicking on the line between them.

Final image
With the sky slightly darker and the poppies popping, this image has a completely different feel. When you're finished, it's a good idea to save the image as a Photoshop file (PSD), as well as a JPEG or TIFF, so you can come back to the picture at any point and re-edit the layers.

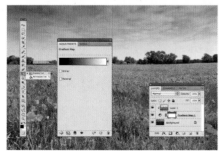

6 Apply the gradient Select the *Gradient Tool* and then the Layer Mask. Holding down **Shift**, click and drag the tool from the top of the image to where the foreground begins. Repeat until you find the right balance between land and sky.

7 Global adjustments Combine all the layers into a new layer (see Secrets Unlocked, right) so you can now make global adjustments with *Contrast/Brightness* and *Saturation* to breathe a bit more life into the picture.

Secrets unlocked

✓ COMBINE IMAGE LAYERS

If you're working with an image with multiple layers, usually you have to merge the layers together to make any global adjustments – unless you know this trick. Click on the top layer in the Layers palette and press **Shift**, **Ctrl**, **Alt** and the **E** key (PC) or **Shift**, **Cmd**, **Alt** and **E** (Mac). By doing so, you combine all the layers below it to create one image layer, without having to flatten or merge all your layers together. This way you can go back and still edit the individual layers if you want.

Bland to beautiful: learn how to replace a sky

Improve your landscape images ten-fold with this simple technique where you can swap an uninspiring sky for one with more drama

Jordan Butters: The British weather is well known for not doing quite what you want it to and rarely do all of the elements play ball when it comes to landscape photography. You can be perched above a beautiful vista, camera-ready on a tripod and remote in hand, but the one thing you can't do much about is a bland sky. All is not lost, though: in a few simple Photoshop steps you can replace the sky and transform your landscapes from drab to dramatic. You'll need to find a replacement sky to swap in, of course, and it's worth keeping a small library of skies in a folder on your computer for such occasions.

Try to shoot a range of different skies from different times of the day: the benefit of this is that it makes it a lot easier when the sky you are replacing is of a similar colour and time of the day to the replacement. You'll often find that trial and error is the key to finding the right sky for your scene.

1 Select the sky Open your image, choose the *Quick Selection Tool* and begin painting across the sky. If your image contains objects on the horizon, as ours does, you will need to zoom in and adjust your brush *Size* in the options toolbar to make a more accurate selection. If you select an area by mistake, simply hold down the *Alt* key and erase the selection. Once happy with your selection, go to *Select>Inverse*.

2 Refine the selection Go to *Select>Refine Edge* to bring up the Options window. Click *Default* and the sky will appear white. Using the *Contract/Expand* slider, adjust the selection so that it closely follows the lines of the horizon. You can alter the preview that you see by selecting one of the preview options at the bottom. Once done, click *OK*. Then go to *Select>Inverse* again and press the *Backspace* key to remove the sky.

3 Bring in the new sky Open your replacement sky image in a new window and, using the *Rectangular Marquee Tool*, select the sky only. Copy your selection by going to *Edit>Copy* and close your sky image without saving. Head back to your original image and paste the sky in by going to *Edit>Paste*. It's very unlikely that your new sky will fit your image straight away, so don't worry if this is the case.

4 Adjust the proportions Go to *Edit> Transform>Scale* and, holding down the *Shift* key, drag the corners of the sky image out to match the width of your landscape. Once happy, click on the *Tick* at the top, or press the *Enter* key. Use the *Move Tool* to line the sky up so that it completely covers the white area of the image. Don't worry about any overlap onto the horizon at this point.

5 Create a gradient Click on the *Add Vector Mask* button in the Layers palette. Select the *Gradient Tool* and, at the top of the screen, make sure that the black to white gradient is selected. On the image, click and drag the line from just below the horizon towards the top of the sky, then release the button. This part involves some trial and error, but you can repeat as many times as you need to until you are happy with the effect.

✓ New horizons
The sky typically gets brighter the closer to the horizon it is. Bear this in mind when applying your gradient – if the gradient is too low or too hard, then the effect will lack realism

Final image
We think you'll agree that the new sky adds some much needed drama to the original image.

ISTOCK PHOTO

6 Tidy up the horizon Some of your new sky will still overlap onto the landscape, so to tidy this up, select the *Brush Tool*, lower the *Opacity* to *25%* and set the brush's *Hardness* to *25%* in the brush options toolbar. Select *Black* as your *Foreground color* and brush over the horizon, building up areas that you wish to reveal. If you go too far or make a mistake, simply select *White* as your *Foreground color* and brush back over.

7 Adjust the contrast In the Layers palette, click on the *Create new adjustment layer* button and select *Levels* from the menu. First make sure that the adjustment is clipped to the layer below only by clicking the button at the bottom of the Adjustments palette. Then adjust the contrast of your sky to match the rest of the image using the middle (mid-tones) level slider. Once done, save your image using *File>Save As*.

Secrets unlocked

✓ **QUICK SELECTION**

The Quick Selection Tool was released with the launch of Photoshop CS3 and Elements 6, and has featured in all versions since. It works by detecting contrast differences, and makes a selection based on this; ideal for separating skies from horizons. Just be aware of horizons with low cloud or mist cover, as the tool may struggle to separate them accurately.

How to create a digital panoramic

A simple but effective technique to expand your photo's field of view

Lee Frost: The theory is simple: shoot a load of overlapping pictures, then join them together on your computer. In the past this would have needed specialist software, but now Photoshop and Elements will give you great results.

Shooting the individual frames that you'll be splicing together is something that's important to get right. You'll need a tripod (if you are shooting a distant landscape this doesn't have to be a specialist panoramic model) and a spirit level to get things straight. Set an average exposure that is good for the whole scene and lock this in using manual exposure mode, so the exposure doesn't change between frames.

When you're back at base, it's then a case of taking those individual shots into Photoshop and using the Photomerge command to kick off the merging step. It's an intuitive process that will produce an image that you can fine-tune further using Photoshop's normal editing tools.

1 Set up Mount your camera on a tripod in vertical format and make sure the tripod base is even, so that way when you rotate the camera between shots it remains level. Do a quick practice scan across the scene to decide where your panorama will begin and end.

2 Use manual mode Take a test shot from an average part of the scene – not the lightest or the darkest. Check the image and histogram, and if all looks OK, dial in that exposure with your camera in manual mode, so you use exactly the same settings for each frame.

3 Set the starting point Swing the camera to the far left of the view you want to capture, focus manually, and take a shot of your left hand with your fingers pointing to the right. This denotes where the sequence begins so you don't get confused later on.

4 Get the shots Take the first shot of the sequence, move the camera slightly to the right and make your second exposure. Repeat this until you reach the other end of the scene, making sure you overlap each image by 30-40% to enable easy stitching later.

5 Take the closing shot Take a shot of your right hand with your fingers pointing to the left to denote the end of the sequence. When you download the files to your computer you'll know that all the images between the two hand shots are in the same sequence.

Final image
The result is a stunning panorama created from eight individual images, stitched in Photoshop CS3. The finished 16-bit, 280MB TIFF file is good for prints up to 90cm long, at 300dpi, and that's without any interpolation!

Which Photoshop?

✓ PHOTOSHOP CS4/CS5
£600 / PC & Mac
This may seem rather an expensive option, purely to do photo stitching – even at the cheaper upgrade price – but the Photomerge tool in CS4 and CS5 is unbelievably good, even with the most complex of stitches. Obviously, you will get much more out of it than just stitching, but if you are starting to take your photography seriously, you will not be disappointed at the potential of either version. Alternatively, you may be able to pick up a cheaper version of CS3 that still has an impressive stitcher, too!

✓ ELEMENTS 10
£65 / PC & Mac
If your budget won't stretch to CS5, don't worry. The latest versions of Elements are also equipped with all the tools you need for an impressive and hassle-free stitch. Elements 6 onwards include the Photomerge command (found under *File>New>Photomerge Panorama*) and appear to do an equally good job at blending and adjusting images for a panorama – at least to the same standard as CS3. However, it doesn't have some of the improved functionality of CS4/5's Photomerge.

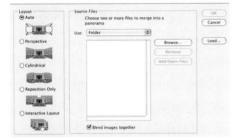

6 Batch process the files Download the images to a computer. If you shoot in Raw, batch process the Raw files from the sequences so they all receive the same adjustments and corrections, otherwise inconsistencies will creep in. Place those images in a folder.

7 Access Photomerge Open Photoshop and go to *File>Automate>Photomerge*. Select the layout style you desire. Auto usually works fine. You may like to also try Cylindrical and Perspective. Click on the *Use* tab, select *Folders* then click on *Browse*.

8 Merge the files Click on the folder containing the images you want to stitch and they will appear in the Photomerge dialogue box. Click *OK* and let Photomerge perform its magic. This can take a few minutes, so put the kettle on and make yourself a cuppa!

9 Crop to complete Once your stitch is complete, you may need to use the *Crop Tool* to tidy up the edges. This is common if you don't use a Nodal Point bracket to eliminate parallax error, but it's nothing to worry about. Only a few more tweaks and you're finished!

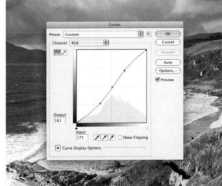

10 Merge the files After saving the stitch and flattening the layers (*Layer>Flatten Image*), make any further adjustments until you're happy with the overall look of the image and remove any distracting elements with the *Clone Stamp Tool*. Job done!

Original

Edited

Learn how to revive your old photographs in a few steps

Restoring images is a doddle, it's retaining their charm that's the challenge. Here's all you need to know to make yours look like new

Caroline Wilkinson: Most of us would admit to having family photos, generations old, gathering dust in a drawer, too damaged to display. Before they get beyond repair, take the time to digitalise them by scanning the prints into a computer to do some restoration work. Then burn them to a disc, save them to your hard drive, put the old prints into archival protective sleeves and frame the new images. It's a lengthy process, but you'll be preserving the memories for generations to come.

Before I go further, we advise you don't cut corners on the printing of your new images. Use archival quality inks and papers to avoid discolouration and fading over time. Files corrupt and formats change, so make sure you have quality hard copies, too. If your archived images never made it into prints, remaining as 35mm slides or

negatives, you can still digitalise the pictures by using a flatbed scanner.

You may be tempted to convert old prints to black & white, but part of the charm is their aged, sepia cast. It can cause images to look dull and flat, so reducing any cast will be a benefit, but getting rid of it entirely isn't restoring the images sympathetically.

Here, I used Selective Color to reduce yellow and red tones in the colour channels, Whites and Neutrals (mid-tones), but you could try Color Balance or Hue/Saturation. Dust, scratches, creases and stains are common with old photos; most can be cleared up using the Dust and Scratches command, but at the expense of softening details, which is why sharpening the image is another crucial step. You can then use the Healing Brush Tool for minor damage and the Clone Stamp Tool for areas of major restoration.

How to scan the image

If you have Photoshop, you can import your image directly.

☑ 1) IMPORT:

In Photoshop, go to *File* and choose *Import>Twain Acquire* (Mac) or *WIA Support* (PC) to open the scanning software. Make sure *Open Acquired Images* is selected and choose *Adjust the Quality of The Scanned Picture*.

☑ 2) SETTINGS:

Select the appropriate dpi by estimating the scan resolution. The minimum resolution you should set when scanning an image for print is 300dpi and for every doubling in print size, double the dpi – ie if you scan a 4x6in print but want to print the image, double the size (8.5x11in) and double the resolution (300dpi to 600dpi). Also scan the image in at 200% to improve image quality when the picture is enlarged. Saving the file as a TIFF will also help. Press *Preview* to trial the scan and use the selection tool to crop the image to the proper size, ready for the actual scan.

☑ 3) CROP:

In Photoshop, use the *Crop Tool* to do any cropping and straightening.

1 **Prepare your picture** With your image imported and cropped in Photoshop, duplicate the image by dragging the *Background layer* down to the *Create a new layer* icon at the bottom of the Layers palette (accessible via *Windows>Layers*).

2 **Adjust the colour** Add a Selective Color adjustment layer (*Layer>New Adjustment Layer>Selective Color*) and then in the *Colors* drop-down menu, select *Reds* and adjust the sliders to reduce the sepia tint. Do the same for *Neutral* and *Whites*.

3 **Adjust the contrast** Use a *Levels* adjustment layer to improve the tonal range globally. Next, click on a duplicate image layer and use the Dodge and Burn tools to make localised tonal adjustments, keeping the *Exposure* below *10*, the brush's *Hardness* to *0* and vary the *Range*.

4 **Retouch marks** Select all the layers by holding down *Shift* and clicking on each. Then press *Cmd+Alt+Shift+E* to create a combined layer. Go to *Filter>Convert to Smart Filters*, then *Filter>Noise>Dust and Scratches*. Keep the *Radius* to *1px* and *Threshold 0*.

5 **Sharpen the image** As scanning and Dust and Scratches softens a lot of the detail, you need to sharpen the image slightly. With the 'combined' layer selected, go to *Filter>Sharpen> Unsharp Mask* and adjust the *Radius* slider, being watchful of artefacts affecting image quality.

6 **Clone and Heal** Duplicate the 'combined' layer by dragging it down to the *Create New Layer* icon in the Layers palette. Now zoom into the image 100% and work your way around using the *Healing Brush* to get rid of any marks or stains. Use the *Clone Stamp* on edges to avoid blurring.

Add a creative lens flare effect

Captured a shot that's missing that extra bit of punch? See how adding a faux lens flare in Photoshop can add interest to your images

Jordan Butters: Lens flare is caused by harsh light entering your lens and bouncing between the lens elements. The results vary from colourful circles of light scattered across your image to reduced contrast, overexposed areas and colour casts. On the surface they all sound like the kind of thing we strive to avoid in our photographs, but half the fun of photography is in bending the rules.

Lens flare can add great atmosphere and a summer feel to an image. Capturing flare intentionally in-camera is relatively straightforward – however, controlling flare so that it doesn't detract from your image is another matter altogether. Thankfully, lens flare is relatively straightforward to recreate using Photoshop.

Lens flare is one of those elements that very much depends on the type of image it is being applied to; it certainly won't work for all pictures. It is a warm, soft effect so tends to suit outdoor portraits of women and children very well. It's also an effect that has to be applied with caution, as incorrect placement

of the flare can completely spoil an image. It works best when applied to photographs whereby your light source is above and behind your subject – for example, when the sun is low in the sky, such as during early morning or late afternoon. If you apply lens flare to an image in which the sun is directly overhead, the direction of the shadows in the image will contradict the direction that the flare is coming from, instantly discrediting the effect. Therefore, before you start editing your image, the most important step is to identify the direction that the light is coming from. Look at the direction of any shadows for clues or for areas of light and dark on your subject. Always apply the flare to complement the direction of the natural light.

Furthermore, this is one of those effects that should be applied with restraint. The temptation is always there to crank the sliders all the way across for the most dramatic effect, but the further you push the parameters, the less realistic the effect will appear. If done right, the viewer shouldn't be able to tell that the flare isn't all natural.

Original

1 Create a layer for the flare Create a blank new layer for your flare by going to *Layer>New>Layer*. In the New Layer dialogue box that opens, change the *Blend Mode* to *Screen* and tick the *Fill with Screen-neutral colour* (black) checkbox. Click *OK* to create the layer.

2 Add the flare Go to *Filter>Render>Lens Flare* to open the Lens Flare dialogue box. Click on the black thumbnail window to set the position of the flare in relation to your image and select your choice of flare and *Brightness*, I have chosen 50-300mm Zoom at 165%. Click *OK*.

3 Create an Adjustment Layer In the Layers palette, click on the *Add new fill or adjustment layer* button and select *Hue/Saturation*. Go to *Layer>Create Clipping Mask* to clip the Adjustment Layer to the lens flare layer only.

4 Adjust the Hue In the Adjustments palette, click the *Colorize* check box and change the *Hue* and the *Saturation*. I found setting the Hue to around 45 and Saturation to around 60 gives the flare a warmer, more realistic cast.

5 Add a Layer Mask If any flare artefacts are distracting or cover important areas of your image, click on the flare layer in the Layers palette before clicking on the *Add layer mask* button. Select the *Brush Tool* and adjust the *Opacity* to *50%* at the top menu bar.

6 Remove distractions Make sure that your *Foreground color* is set to *Black* and paint over any areas of flare that you wish to remove from the image. If you go a step too far, switch your *Foreground color* to *White* and brush back over.

Control your viewers' gaze by adding a vignette

Maximise the impact of your pictures by rounding off with this classic technique – a very simple trick to make your subject stand out…

Original

Caroline Wilkinson: How to take your images from good to great, quite frankly, could simply be a few tweaks in Photoshop. A test of a great picture is how well it contains your eye within the frame: the longer you can control the viewers' gaze, the more engaging the image. While composition plays a big part in this, adding a vignette can help, too. Essentially, the technique is to gradually reduce the image's brightness from the centre (focal point), fading off toward the edges, creating a border around the subject and drawing the eye towards the point of interest.

While some photographers do whatever they can to avoid lens vignetting, if the effect is controlled for creative effect and used on an appropriate picture – like this one where the focal point is central in the frame – it can have massive impact. It can be as subtle or as strong as you like, but some of the most appealing vignettes have a very soft graduation and edges that blend with the image for a natural finish.

Anyone that worked in the darkroom will know that vignetting is not a digital technique – in fact, it's been around since the dawn of photography – though there are now countless methods of creating one, each with differing effects. For now, try this modern version of the darkroom classic – you'll be surprised at what a difference it makes.

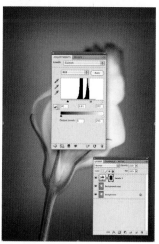

1 Create a copy Make any adjustments you need to before finishing the image with a vignette. First, copy the image by going to *Layer>Duplicate Layer* or drag the *Background Layer* down to the *Create a new layer* icon at the bottom of the Layers palette.

2 Draw your vignette Select the *Rectangular Marquee Tool* and click and drag the marquee over the area you want to frame, or, in other words, your focal point. To soften the edge of the vignette, go to *Select>Modify>Feather* and type in *250px*, then click *OK*.

3 Invert the selection At the moment, any adjustments you make will affect the area within the marquee selection, which is not what you want. To target the area outside of the marquee, creating a frame around your focal point, go to *Select>Inverse*.

4 Darken the edges Add a Levels adjustment layer (*Layer>New Adjustment Layer>Levels*) and slowly drag the black and grey triangle sliders to the right to darken the corners until you reach your desired effect. Once you're done, go to *Select>Deselect*.

Blend Modes

Try changing the Blend Mode of your Levels adjustment layer for different results. Click on the *Levels* adjustment layer in the Layers palette and select the *Blend Mode* drop-down menu at the top of the Layers palette. Experiment with the different modes and try reducing the strength of the effect by reducing the *Opacity* slider for the Levels layer. Here are three of our favourite Blend Modes…

Hard light

Multiply

Soft light

Final image
The beauty of this technique is it darkens the colour gradually from the outer edges of the image, drawing the eye towards your point of interest.

Add texture to photographs

Mastering the fundamentals of Layers, Layer Masks and Blend Modes creates new possibilities for post-production. Find out how to combine all three to apply textures and add impact to your pictures

Caroline Wilkinson: Adding texture to a photograph can produce beautifully artistic effects and, while the results may look complicated, it's relatively simple to achieve a strong finish. The principle behind it is mastering how to blend layers together by becoming accustomed with the various methods of doing so, as each one produces a different end result.

Textures aren't something that should be used recklessly: it's easy to allow them to overwhelm a perfectly good picture. Your choice of texture should work with the image to enhance its mood, colour and, ultimately, impact. However, picked carefully they can add character to an ordinary snapshot and improve a picture's appeal tenfold.

To truly understand how this technique works, the *Photoshop Fundamentals* section at the front of this MagBook explains in-depth how Layers, Layer Masks and Blend Modes work together. As an outline, though, when applying a texture, make sure it's on top of the image layer in the Layers palette for it to affect the image. You can then use the Opacity slider at the top of the Layers palette to control the transparency of the texture and/or apply a Blend Mode from the drop-down menu at the top of the Layers palette. In general, we've found that Multiply, Screen, Soft Light and Overlay work the best when merging layers. There are no rules for how many layers you should use, but the more you do apply, the more the original character of the image will be altered.

HOW TO USE

Layer Masks
A Layer Mask allows you to hide detail from the layer it's applied to, revealing the image beneath without erasing it. When the Layer Mask is selected, simply add the colour **Black** to the mask to hide image detail and change to the colour **White** to restore the detail. Use the **X** key to quickly switch between the colours.

HOT KEY

Changing Blend Modes

To quickly apply Blend Modes, hold down **Shift** and press **+** and **–** keys to move up and down the list respectively. Or, for an even quicker way, press **Alt/ Option+Shift** and the letter for that particular Blend Mode, eg **O** for Overlay or **S** for Soft Light.

Original

ISTOCKPHOTO

Final image
Choosing textures that enhance the warm colours of the original image complement the image as well as creating a painterly effect.

1 Open your image Duplicate your photograph (*Layer>Duplicate Layer*) and open your first textured layer. I've used a picture of sandstone as the colour complements the autumn tones and the cracks make good texture. Click on and drag the textured image layer on to the image layer using the **Move Tool**.

2 Transform the texture Go to *Edit>Free Transform*, hold **Shift** to constrain the proportions and drag a corner widget outwards to meet the sides of your image. Press the **Tick** to commit to the adjustment. Change the texture layer's **Blend Mode** to merge it with the image layer. Here, Overlay was used to boost saturation.

3 Add a Layer Mask As the texture flows over the face, it can start to obscure the features. Apply a Layer Mask to the texture layer by clicking on **Create layer mask** at the bottom of the Layers palette. Select the **Brush Tool** and set a soft-edge brush with **Opacity** set low, then using **Black** paint, brush over the face to reduce the texture.

4 **Add more texture** Repeat steps one to three with another texture and try out the different Blend Modes to see their effects. Here, Multiply was used to emphasise the lines in the tree texture. If the resulting texture is still slightly too strong, try reducing the layer's *Opacity* using the slider at the top of the Layer's palette.

5 **Repeat the steps** There's no rule for what textures work and how many you should use; the key is trial and error and building up the effect gradually. Here, four textures are layered, each with different Blend Modes and varying opacity. Moving the layers in different positions within the Layers palette can also change the result.

Secrets unlocked

☑ WHERE CAN YOU GET TEXTURES?

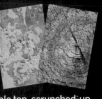

The easiest way to get texture images is to photograph them yourself: it's so easy to do and you can find them anywhere, be it a brick wall, granite table top, scrunched-up paper or flaky paint on a wall. Textures are everywhere. Your other option is to download them from the internet. Sites such as deviantart.com, textureking. com and amazingtextures.com are good sources, but a quick Google search will uncover hundreds of options.

Composite subjects with fine hair

Wispy strands of hair are a headache to select even for the seasoned Photoshop user, but this simple step-by-step technique should make the process a lot smoother and give a really good result

Luke Marsh: If you've ever tried to composite a person on to a different background, then you'll know that the hair can be the hardest area to select. Extracting the fine, flyaway strands can be frustrating and time-consuming, but crucial if you want your composite to look seamless and not like a hard-edged helmet.

The success of this technique depends on the type of background you're extracting from and it's a lot easier if the subject is against a grey or white backdrop, or one that's uniform and light in tone. If it's not uniform, you could use the Brush Tool to paint the background white.

Workflow tools

✓ DIFFERENT BACKGROUNDS!

Creating a Layer Mask that works well with fine hair can be time-consuming, but once it's done, pretty much any background can be dropped in without the need for further editing. Simply reveal the silhouette layer hidden in step seven by clicking on the eye icon, then repeat the instructions from step five to step eight, using your replacement background accordingly.

1 Duplicate layer Create a copy of your image layer (*Layer>New>Layer via Copy*), then go to *Image>Adjustments>Desaturate* to remove the colour from this new layer. Next, go to *Image> Adjustments>Levels...* and move the black slider right to no more than *100* for lighter hair or no more than *50* for dark or black hair. This process is to darken the hair significantly, the hair strands don't need to be perfectly black at this stage.

2 Brush the edges Select the *Brush Tool* set to *Black*, with a medium-sized, soft edge and with the *Mode* set to *Overlay* in the Options bar. Now, brush around the edge of the model to darken areas missed by Levels. The brush will darken areas of the subject while the white background will remain unaffected. Don't go over any areas of fine hair yet as this is best done gradually with reduced opacity to avoid problems.

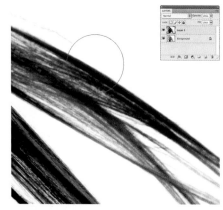

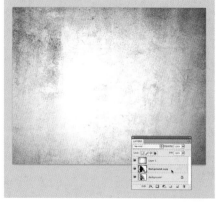

3 Darken the fine hair Reduce the brush *Opacity* to *50%* in the Options bar then, using the same principle as before, work over the hair strands to darken them. The reduced opacity will help to build up the effect, especially on very fine hair strands. Don't attempt to get the strands completely black at this stage as this can thicken them irreversibly. Once the background is added, final tweaks can be made to perfect the strands.

4 Fill the gaps Now the edges of the image have been darkened, it's time to fill in detail in the centre. Change the brush's *Mode* to *Normal* and *Opacity* to *100%*, and begin to fill any areas of detail that remain. As the brush is now set to Normal, be sure to work at the centre of the subject, and prevent your strokes from overlapping into the white areas of the image. You should now have a perfect silhouette of your hair image.

5 Add a background Open your background file and go to *Select>All* then *Edit>Cut* to copy the image. Go back to your hair file and click *Edit>Paste* to place the background image at the top of the Layers palette and resize the image if necessary. Click on the hair silhouette layer beneath, go to *Select>All* and then *Edit>Copy* to place the silhouette on to the pasteboard. Now click back on the background image layer above.

Final image
A perfect process that will take you one step closer to creating elaborate composites.

6 Add a Layer Mask Add a Layer Mask to the background image by going to *Layer>New Layer Mask>Reveal All* – the Layer Mask will appear next to the image thumbnail in the Layers palette. Hold the *Alt* key and click on the *Layer Mask*: the screen will go blank to show that the content of the mask is empty. Now go to *Edit>Paste* to place the hair silhouette into the Layer Mask. It will also appear on the blank screen.

7 View the effect The original silhouette layer has served its purpose so hide it by clicking on its eye icon in the Layers palette. Hold down *Alt* and click on the *Layer Mask* attached to the background layer to hide the preview. You will now see a rough composite of the hair and background image. The hair at this stage is looking good but by no means perfect. Change the *Blend Mode* to *Multiply* to improve the composite further.

8 Final tweaks With the Layer Mask active, open *Image>Adjustments>Levels...* and move the grey slider left while previewing the results on the image. Stop when you feel the hair strands are almost perfect without any halos appearing around them. Finally, using the *Brush Tool*, with the *Mode* set to *Overlay* and the colour to *Black*, work over any remaining imperfections, which tend to be in areas of very fine hair.

Creating movement

Having trouble panning moving subjects? Want a quick-fire way to add movement to your pictures? Then you need the Motion Blur filter

Luke Marsh: The Motion Blur filter can be used to add the illusion of movement to a static subject by simulating a linear blur in any direction. It's a basic filter to use, but highly effective, and can be used for various effects. Once you select the filter, it opens up a control panel with a preview screen and features that enable you to specify the angle of the blur to match the direction of the 'moving' subject.

The Distance slider varies the strength of the blur to simulate speed. When the subject is moving towards the camera, Radial Blur's Zoom mode works better than the Motion Blur filter, but for this technique, you'll also need to use Radial Blur's Spin mode to add movement to the wheels. It's tricky, but effective, so give it a go.

1 Make a selection Using the *Polygonal Lasso Tool*, take time to make a careful selection around the edge of the car. Now use *Select>Inverse* to flip the selection, selecting the background of the image rather than the subject.

2 Isolate the background To copy this selection to a new layer go to *Layer>New> Layer via Copy*. This layer now contains the background that will be blurred to add the illusion of movement, while the car remains sharp.

3 Lock transparent pixels Before adding blur, click the *Lock transparent pixels* icon (circled). This will ensure that any blur effect will run to the edge of the transparent areas, seen on the preview as a white and grey checkered pattern.

4 Apply Motion Blur Open *Filter>Blur>Motion Blur*. In the window, move the *Angle* control to match the direction of the subject – try to find the most realistic angle of motion. Then increase *Distance* until satisfied with the effect.

5 Select the rear wheel Click on the *Background Layer* in the Layers palette. Now make a selection around the rear wheel and feather the selection by a small amount (*Select>Modify>Feather*) to soften the edge.

Final image
It takes patience and practice, but the effect is effective when done well.

6 Apply Radial Blur For the appearance of spinning wheels, use Radial Blur (*Filter>Blur> Radial Blur*). Set the *Quality* to *Best* and set an *Amount* of no more than *15-20* pixels. *Blur Center* should be moved to match the centre of the wheel.

7 Blur the front wheel Repeat this process for the front wheel. Make a feathered selection, then apply *Radial Blur* as before. The only thing that may change here is the position of the Blur Center, which will most likely be different.

8 Save the layers A file containing multiple layers cannot be saved as a JPEG, therefore it's always advisable to use *File>Save* to save a copy as a Photoshop file (PSD). This will preserve the layers, allowing for editing later on.

Learn how to retouch your portraits like a pro

Always wanted to create polished portraits like the professionals? Well, now's your chance. The best-kept secrets of retouching are disclosed in this guide from some of the world's leading retouchers – read on to find out how to enhance the natural beauty of your subjects with expert tutorials and advice

OFTEN THE DIFFERENCE between average portraits and the polished images that you see by high-end pros or in glossy magazines is not only photographic prowess, but the skill of the retoucher, or lack thereof. In many respects, the taking of a portrait is just one step towards a finished picture, but great lighting and photography are fundamental as Photoshop is not a miracle worker: it's an enhancement tool – and a powerful one at that. It can transform good photos to great images with impact, but you need a quality picture to begin with to get the most from post-production. While how you originally light the subject doesn't affect retouching, the lighting should be as close as you can get it to the finished look and your exposure needs to be spot-on: if you can get the skin looking light and bright, rather than a muddy tone, retouching is going to be a lot easier. If you have to lighten up pixels, you'll have noise issues, the colour won't be as good and it'll take a lot longer to get a half-decent result. Some photographers mistakenly start with a bad image, thinking they can transform it in Photoshop, but apply so much manipulation that the picture loses any sense of realism.

There are some other things you can do to make retouching easier. Make sure you shoot in Raw rather than JPEG. Make-up is helpful, too: apply foundation that's the right tone for the skin to avoid any lines between the face and neck, as well as a light dusting of powder to get rid of shine caused by the heat of the studio lights. Lipstick should be applied perfectly: make sure the lips are sculpted properly and there's no bleeding over the edges of the mouth and the eye make-up shapes the eyes. Lighting and smoothing are essential for beautiful hair. Split ends are a nightmare to retouch, so try to make sure the hair is in good condition before you start and preferably lit well to create highlights. The more highlights there are to begin with, the easier they will be to draw out during editing.

Before you start retouching, you need to calibrate your monitor (we'd recommend X-Rite's i1Match, Datacolor's Spyder4ELITE or Pantone hueyPRO for easy-to-use calibration devices). Skipping this step could mean your printed image looks nothing like it did on screen and those hours of colour refinement and tonal tweaks were wasted. Then plan what you want to do to the image – it should stop you from over- or under-processing areas – make yourself a coffee and be prepared for a long time in front of your monitor. The most polished and subtle retouching takes an abundance of time, an eye for detail and plenty of patience to ensure natural-looking results. Retouching is not about changing a model beyond recognition or transforming them into a Barbie doll; you should be trying to enhance features and work with the person's natural beauty so the portrait presents the very best version of them and improves the overall image impact.

Start by assessing the overall quality of the skin: blemishes, under-eye 'bags', how even the colour is, the cleanliness of the make-up,

Original

deep-set wrinkles, crow's feet and unwanted highlights created by shiny skin. Next, address the features: do the eyebrows need to be neatened? Can the shape be improved or stray hairs eliminated? Could the eyes be brightened and the colour intensified? Is the nose too wide or the teeth a little stained? There is so much that can be refined that even small tweaks make a huge improvement.

For the final image to look great, you need to work on the details, and that means zooming in and working on areas of pixels close up. Use lots of layers, but keep them organised and remember to save, save, save: it's easy to get engrossed and forget. Once you're finished, save the layered image as a PSD file in case you want to come back to it, but also flatten the layers (*Image>Flatten Image*) and save the image as a TIFF to compress the enormous file size for print. *This article was produced with the advice and insight of professional retouchers Fay Bacon, Amy Dresser and Chanelle Segerius-Bruce.*

Hair

Get glossy, healthy hair with this simple tutorial

YOU'D BE AMAZED at the time it takes to retouch hair at a professional standard; we're talking days or weeks for those retouchers preparing a picture for a shampoo commercial or competition. For straight hair, they would literally have to clone each stray hair so it was straight using a very hard 2px brush set to 100% Opacity. You also have to reduce the amount of flyaway hairs to smooth out the surface, but if you eliminate too many, the hair can end up looking like a helmet.

To make the hair look fuller and thicker, some retouchers may even composite hair from various different shots into the picture and morph them together using layers and Layer Masks. It can be a huge amount of work, which is why we've picked up a few tips from our professional contributors, including retoucher Chanelle Segerius-Bruce (www.retouchme.co.uk), who has retouched images for Pantene campaigns and The Body Shop.

Neatening up hair

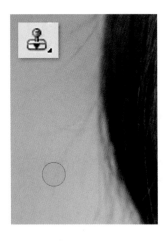

To reduce those niggly little flyaway strands and smooth out the surface of the hair, start by adding an empty new layer and set the layer's *Blend Mode* to *Darken*. Now select the *Clone Stamp Tool*, set the *Hardness* to *100%*, *Opacity* to *100%* and the *Blend Mode* to *Darken*, too. Use a small brush, big enough to cover the strand of hair, and take a sample from the area just next to it and clone over the strand. While the Darken blend mode works on light flyaway hairs, if the strands are dark, set the *Blend Mode* for the layer and brush to *Lighten* instead. To get rid of hairs entirely, use the same technique by setting the *Blend Mode* to *Normal*.

Change hair colour

Only alter colour a few shades from the original: dramatic changes make it difficult to target flyaway strands

1) The easiest way to select the hair is to use Quick Mask Mode (*Select>Edit in Quick Mask Mode*) and 'paint' over the hair area. When you're done, click *Select>Edit in Quick Mask Mode* again to remove the red mask and reveal the selection.

2) Create a new layer and use the *Brush Tool* loaded with your choice of colour. 'Paint' over the selection onto the empty new layer and change the *Blend Mode* to *Soft Light* to merge the colour with the texture and natural colour of the hair.

3) The tricky part is when it comes to targeting missed stray hairs of the original colour. Zoom in close and use a small brush to edit the obvious hairs and then use a Layer Mask to remove colour where needed.

Want shampoo commercial-worthy hair? Then follow these few easy steps...

1) Boost contrast Add a *Curves* adjustment layer and boost the contrast (concentrating on bringing out the natural highlights in the hair), click *OK*. Now invert the attached Layer Mask (*command+I*) to fill it with Black, hiding the adjustment.

2) Refine Using the *Brush Tool* on the Layer Mask, 'paint' over the natural highlights to strengthen them. Reduce the *Opacity* slider for the adjustment layer if needed and switch the layer's visibility on and off to see the effects and to help assess the highlights.

3) Dodge Next, duplicate the image layer and select the *Dodge Tool*. With a large brush, target the highlights with an *Exposure* of *10-15%*, varying the *Range* between *Midtones* and *Highlights*. Reduce the layer's *Opacity* slider if you overdo it slightly.

4) Sharpen Duplicate the layer again and apply a *High Pass filter* (*Filter>High Pass*) set to *5px* and change the layer's *Blend Mode* to *Soft Light*. As High Pass can be a little harsh on skin, add a *Layer Mask* and hide the skin, leaving only the hair looking crisper.

Body shape

Learn the trade tricks for sculpting a body with Liquify

LIQUIFY IS USUALLY the first tool to hand for retouchers wanting to edit a person's body, whether it be shrinking or elongating a waist, increasing breast or bicep size, slimming legs or lumps and bumps. High-end retoucher Fay Bacon (www.celebritypublicity.co.uk / www.ukmodelfolios.co.uk), who has worked on images of models for many high-profile photographers, explains how she performs subtle body sculpting.

Elongate legs

1) Lengthen legs: To elongate the legs, select the bottom half of the image beneath the knees using the *Rectangular Marquee Tool* and then go to *Edit>Transform* and pull the whole image down to extend it while keeping the natural proportions. In this image, there wasn't enough space between the feet and the bottom part of the picture, so I increased the height of the canvas (*Image>Canvas Size*) by 4cm, then lengthened the legs. You also need to be careful not to distort the background if it's busy, as you may be forced to rebuild it using the Clone Stamp Tool if it stretches too much.

Original

Edited

2) A nip and tuck: Open the image in *Liquify*, set the brush *Size* to around *300*, *Density* to *12* and *Pressure* to *54*, then using the *Forward Warp Tool*, push the lines of the legs and thighs in to slim them a little. Then push in the waist on either side and push down the area between the neck and shoulder (the slimmer you are, the more this area naturally curves). Then shrink the brush *Size* and concentrate around the tops of the arms and elbow to make them appear slightly more toned. To correct any mistakes, use the *Reconstruct Tool* to brush over edited areas to revert them back to their original state.

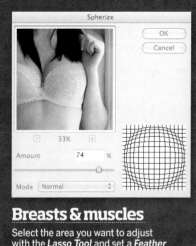

Breasts & muscles

Select the area you want to adjust with the *Lasso Tool* and set a *Feather* of around *20px* to soften the edges of the adjustment. Then go to *Filter> Distort>Spherize* and move the slider to around *50%* to enlarge and lift the selection out of the image for more dimensionality.

Pro tip: Fay Bacon

☑ CLONE STAMP TOOL

If there are body parts you want to adjust that are quite close together (like the arm and the waist), use the *Clone Stamp Tool* to sculpt the area by sampling the background, instead of Liquify, as this can distort the picture. You may need to adjust or add the shadows in the area you've sculpted for it to look natural.

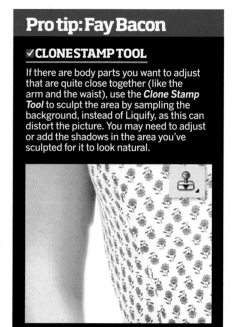

The professional solution

LA-based retoucher Amy Dresser is highly regarded in the industry for her signature style. Here, she reveals her workflow and trade secrets

AMY DRESSER IS A freelance retoucher for numerous professional photographers and, perhaps most notably, was Jill Greenberg's full-time retoucher. Photographers come to her specifically for her signature technique, which she describes as "straddling perfection and realism". While she concentrates on achieving clean skin, she's very careful to retain the reality of the person by using tiny polishing adjustments rather than the grand skin bleaching used by many retouchers.

A lot of her work is based on refining skin colour by making small selections and adjustments using the Red, Green and Blue Channels in a Curves adjustment layer, with the aim to make the skin the same overall tone and saturation for a flawless, even finish.

Amy starts by selecting a 'hero' area on the face – an area she wants to make everything else match – and then uses her fine-tuned eye to target small areas that need to be adjusted, like the pinks of the cheeks or lightness on the forehead. It's this process that sets her apart from many other professional retouchers, as it demands several hours of careful work.

Shooting and processing Raw files gives you a lot more flexibility when it comes to preparing an image for retouching, but for the best results, use Adobe Camera Raw (ACR) to create a solid base, then take it into Photoshop where you can control small sections and add her sought-after professional sheen that makes the face more three-dimensional. To see more of Amy's astonishing work, visit: www.amydresser.com

Original

1 Edit in Raw Start with the *Exposure* slider and work down: *Exposure* and *Fill Light* are the most important to me. There's not a correct adjustment: go with what looks right and gives you a solid start. Adjust the *Temperature* and *Tint* sliders last, as these tend to influence the mood of the image and are more negotiable. If the skin and hair look best at different settings, consider processing two versions and composite the files.

2 Composite with smart objects If the image was processed more than once, you need to combine these separate images into one. To do this, open each file as Smart Objects and drag each exposure on top of the base exposure. Then use a Layer Mask to hide parts of the images you don't want to show. Once finished, press *Shift+Option+Command+E* to combine the files into a new base layer, which you'll use for retouching.

3 Adjust global colour Start with a few global colour adjustments to bring out or minimise details in the skin – both desirable and undesirable. Use what adjustment layer you're comfortable with: I prefer Curves and slightly adjust the RGB and the individual Channels, accessible via the drop-down menu. There's no right or wrong: it's a matter of personal taste. I also slightly desaturated the image using a Hue/Saturation adjustment layer.

Before

After

4 Clone Remove any large distractions, like stray hairs, specks, lint or acne, using the *Clone Stamp Tool* with its *Opacity* set to *100%* on your 'layer to retouch'. Zoom in closer to the image to make precise adjustments easier. Resist the urge to eliminate everything you see, just things that might jump to your attention if you squint or blur your vision. See if you can limit yourself to just five minutes on this step.

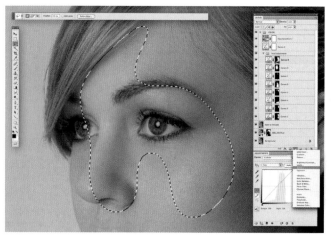

5 **Use Liquify** Tame any bumps in the hair using Liquify's *Forward Warp Tool* (you can also use this on bulges in clothing, too, but avoid using it on people). Use a combination of a big brush with one or two pushes, and smaller brushes with several smaller pushes. It's a very slippery tool, so don't be ashamed to undo (*command+Z*) as often as needed. This step is not always necessary and one I sometimes skip.

6 **Dodge and burn** Refine skin tone and texture using the *Dodge* and *Burn Tools*. Use an ultra-soft brush set to *3% Exposure* and *Range: Midtones*, with *Protect Tones* unticked (CS5 only). 'Dodge' spots and small areas that stand out as being too dark, and 'burn' spots and small areas that stand out as being too light with a brush about the size of the spot. With much larger brushes, use these tools to refine the contours of the face as well.

7 **Local colour adjustments** I like to make my skin tones fairly even in colour, saturation and tone. Create small shifts using the *Lasso Tool* with a large *Feather* (I use around 150px). Circle the area that needs to be adjusted and add a new Adjustment Layer. I prefer adjusting the individual Channels by a notch or two with a Curves adjustment layer. Refine the adjustment to prevent it affecting nearby areas using the attached Layer Mask.

8 **Highlights** Create a new layer set to the default *Normal* blending mode and select the *Brush Tool*, set it to ultra-soft and *White* at *100% Opacity/1% Flow*. Extend and strengthen highlights that are already visible, and with practice you'll be able to create highlights that might be there if another light was added or the subject was shifted slightly. This step will be significantly easier if you use a graphics tablet and a stylus.

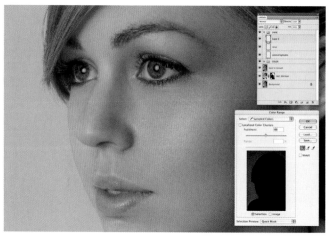

9 **Carving** In a new layer set to *Overlay* blend mode, 'paint' with an ultra-soft brush at *100% Opacity/1% Flow*. Painting with White will create further highlights and painting with Black will create further shading. Brush over the highlights you amplified in the previous step. You can also brush over highlights in the hair and clothing. Switch to *Black* to create extra dimension and depth to the clothing, subject and overall image.

10 **Resample the whites** Create a new blank layer and make sure your *Foreground Color* is *White*. Go to *Select>Color Range* and adjust the *Fuzziness* slider until the selection represents a light dusting of highlights on the subject, and hit *OK*. Fill this selection with White (*Command+delete*) then deselect (*Command+d*). Mask away any areas that have created too heavy a highlight for your liking.

3 Bring the colour back Start 'painting' the larger areas of colour back in, leaving the intricate areas and avoiding the edges of the area you want to colour. Once the main areas are done, go back into the Options bar, pick a smaller brush *Size* and lower the *Hardness* to *25%*.

4 Take your time Zoom in and take your time 'painting' the detailed areas, adjusting the brush Size as needed. Reduce the Hardness further when brushing around the edges. A softer brush creates a softer transition between the colour and black & white that's more pleasing to the eye.

Four seasons

Give your seasonal landscapes a little creative blur for a lot of visual impact. Read on for how to do it…

Caroline Wilkinson: Every season offers new possibilities to photograph striking colour-filled landscapes, whether it be ruby-red poppies, sun-kissed rapeseed, blankets of burnt orange leaves or black & white scenes in winter – you're never short of opportunities. There are a million and one ways to photograph these classic scenes, but this artistic technique can only be done in post-processing. You can create a similar effect in-camera using a three-way pan-tilt tripod head that allows you to move the camera up and down in a fluid movement, but it blurs the whole image, whereas I only want to blur half of it. Plus the effect is much easier to control, with arguably better results, using Photoshop's Motion Blur filter, which is what I'll be using here.

After some trial and error, it was clear that to get the best results, I'd need images where there was as much interest in the top of the frame as the bottom, otherwise you wouldn't be able to tell what was blurred or in focus. The best scenes seemed to be forests or landscapes where trees fill the height of the frame, so with this in mind, I shot some bluebells and started rummaging through my hard drive for suitable images for summer, autumn and winter.

1 Duplicate your image Open your first image in Photoshop and duplicate the image by clicking on the *Background layer* in the Layers palette, then going to *Layer>Duplicate Layer*, or by dragging the *Background layer* down to the *Create a new layer* icon at the bottom of the palette. From now on you'll only be working on this duplicate layer.

2 Apply blur Select the new layer and click *Filter>Blur>Motion Blur* to open the filter's dialogue box. To apply the vertical blur, set the *Angle* to *90º* by typing the amount in or moving the angle finder. By clicking and dragging on the angle finder, the direction of blur will change in the preview.

3 Find the right strength Adjust the *Distance* slider to increase the strength of the effect. The bottom of the image needs to be heavily blurred, but not to the point that the subjects are unrecognisable. It's different for every image, but I stop at 409 pixels. Click *OK*.

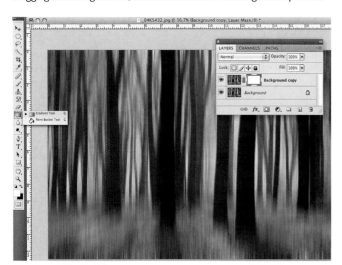

4 Add a Layer Mask Click on the image layer and then on the *Add Layer Mask* icon at the bottom of the Layers palette to add the mask. You'll notice this adds a white box next to your image in the Layers palette. Then select the *Gradient Tool* from the toolbar or press *G*.

5 Apply a gradient Select the *Gradient Tool* and the *Layer Mask* (black lines will appear around the mask's corners when you've got it activated), hover over the image for a cross cursor to appear. Click at the top of the image and drag the cursor down to where you want the blur to start.

Final image
Print the pictures out and frame them for the wall, or why not try having them made into canvas prints or acrylics for a different look?

6 Edit the gradient You've now created a graduated Layer Mask that will hide some of the blur. You can change the graduation by clicking and dragging vertically down the image. You'll find the images look better if the blur is heavier at the bottom of the picture than the top.

7 Finishing touch Repeat steps one to six with the other three images of your choice. I've picked a colourful autumn woodland scene, bright sunshine passing through trees for summer and a black & white picture of a snowy forest. All four look striking on their own, but even better together.

Retro toy camera

Vintage effects are all the rage in photography at the moment: follow our guide to apply a retro toy camera treatment to your images

Jordan Butters: In the past few years, retro photography has taken off in a big way. For many, shooting with film has a nostalgic romance attached to it and so people are seeking to emulate the film look in their digital images. There are apps available for smartphones, such as the popular Hipstamatic and Instagram, which allow you to quickly and easily apply any number of filters to your camera phone snaps – however, as expected, shots from your digital SLR require a little more effort in Photoshop. The benefits of shooting on your DSLR are a higher image quality and more control over both the shot you take and the processing you apply afterwards.

The term 'toy camera' refers to a film camera made almost entirely of plastic, lens included. They are cheap to buy and easy to shoot with, but offer very little in the way of control. Images shot on toy cameras tend to display traits such as oversaturated colours, a sharp image centre with soft edges, heavy vignetting and maybe the occasional light leak. Ironically, the very traits that improvements in technology over the years have eradicated are the ones that the retro photography trend aims to reproduce. The results are visually appealing and the nice thing about this look is that it can be applied to pretty much any kind of photograph, from portraits to cityscapes. Surprisingly, images with visual imperfections such as noise or slight misfocusing often suit the effect better, as this adds to the authenticity of the shot.

Original

1 Crop your image Start by going to *Layer>Duplicate Layer*. Next, crop your image into a square format by selecting the *Crop Tool* and holding down the *Shift* key while selecting an area of your image. Once happy, click on the *Tick* in the top menu bar or press the *Enter* key to commit to the crop.

2 Add a vignette In the Layers palette, right-click on your duplicate layer and select *Convert to Smart Object*. Select *Filter>Lens Correction* and, in the dialogue window that opens, click on the *Custom* tab at the top. In the *Vignette* section, move the *Amount* slider to *-100* and click *OK*.

🔧 Workflow tools

☑ USING THE CURVES TOOL

Photoshop's Curves tool is powerful, but at first glance it can be quite intimidating. Not only does it allow you to tweak contrast as per the Levels tool, but with it you can also adjust how the red, green and blue channels appear independent of one another; perfect for mimicking film effects. The Curves window presents you with a grid with a diagonal line running from the black point of the image in the bottom left to the white point in the top right. The points at which the diagonal line intersects with the grid controls the shadows, the mid-tones and the highlights of your image. The suggestions in our step-by-step are a good start in replicating a retro film effect – however, experimentation is the key. Adjustments to the shape of the curves can completely change the appearance of your image. Thankfully, by using Adjustment Layers, none of the changes are destructive, allowing you to try different settings before settling on one.

3 Add some blur Once back in your main window, go to *Filter>Blur>Gaussian Blur* and, in the Gaussian Blur window that's just opened, set the *Radius* to *13.0* pixels before clicking *OK*. This will blur your entire image. Back in the Layers palette, click on the *Add layer mask* button. Click and hold on the *Paint Bucket Tool* icon to select the *Gradient Tool* and make sure that your *Foreground color* is set to *Black*.

4 Add the edge effects In the menu bar at the top of the screen, click on the *Click to edit the gradient* button and set your gradient as *Foreground to Transparent* from the thumbnail list before clicking *OK*. Select the *Radial Gradient* from the top menu, and click and drag from the centre of your image to one of the corners. You can choose to repeat this action again to create a stronger fall-off in sharpness.

5 Tweak the colours Click on the *Create a new fill or adjustment layer* button in the Layers palette and select *Curves*. In the Adjustments palette, click on the *RGB* menu and select the *Red* channel. Create a shallow 'S'-shaped curve in the Curves window. Select the *Green* channel and apply the same curve. Select the *Blue* channel and create an inverted 'S' curve, as per the image above.

Final image
The final result is a retro-inspired digital image with a vintage toy camera look.

6 **Add light leaks** Click on the *Create new layer* button in the Layers palette, choose the *Gradient Tool* once more and select *Orange* as your *Foreground color.* Click and hold on the artboard off the edge of your image and drag the line into the image to create the gradient. Finally, in the Layers palette, change the *Blend Mode* for the layer to *Vivid Light* and reduce the opacity using the *Opacity* slider.

7 **Draw the border** Go to *Image>Canvas Size* and change the units to *percent*. Set both the *Width* and *Height* to *105* and click *OK* – this will create a border around your image. Click and hold on the *Rectangle Tool* to select the *Rounded Rectangle Tool*. In the top menu bar, first make sure that the *Paths* icon is selected and then set the *Radius* to *200px*. Click and drag from one corner of your image to the other.

8 **Fill the border** Click on *Layer>Flatten Image.* Go into the Paths palette (*Window>Paths*) and click on the *Load path as a selection* button at the bottom to highlight your rounded rectangle selection. Go to *Select>Inverse* before pressing the *Backspace* key to delete the contents of the selection. In the Fill window that opens, set the *Contents* to *White* before clicking *OK*. Finally, click *Select>Deselect*.

Add colour to mono images

Dust off your colouring book skills to transform black & white images

Jordan Butters: Most of us are not strangers to converting images to monochrome. The process can be completed in a matter of seconds with just a few clicks of your mouse. Performing the conversion in the opposite direction is not quite as straightforward, unfortunately, but it is still easily achievable. The main issue is that the colour information is no longer present in the image and therefore the only way to achieve this is to reintroduce the colours manually into areas of the image. This may sound a complicated process, but don't worry – you don't have to be Van Gogh to make this technique work, thanks to the different Blend Modes in Photoshop and Elements. The colouring process can be done in a few simple steps – however, the more care taken, the more convincing the final effect will be. You can apply this technique to images that were shot on black & white film, too – just scan in the photo and use the Dust & Scratches filter and the Healing Brush Tool to tidy up any marks first. As you'll discover, there's something enchanting about seeing an old image converted to colour and given a new lease of life.

Original

TOP TIP...

Blend Modes
Your choice of Blend Mode will affect how each layer of colour is applied to your image. The most useful Blend Modes for this technique are Soft Light and Color. Some experimentation is often required when it comes to applying Blend Modes, as no two modes will offer the exact same effect when applied.

1 Create a new layer To begin, click on the *Create new layer* button in the Layers palette. This layer will contain the base colour for our subject's skin tone. Click on the *Foreground color* icon in the toolbar and use the colour map to choose a suitable skin tone.

2 Add skin colour Select the *Brush Tool* and, in the brush options at the top, set the *Hardness* to *50%* and pick an appropriate brush *Size*. Begin painting over your subject's skin. Do not worry if you go outside of the edges or over facial features as we will correct this later.

Final image
Adding different hues can make an image feel incredibly fresh and vibrant.

3 Change Blend Mode In the Layers palette, change the *Blend Mode* to *Color*. If the skin tone doesn't look realistic, adjust the *Opacity* slider in the Layers palette to desaturate the tone slightly. If this doesn't correct it, try a different foreground colour and repeat the previous step.

4 Add a Layer Mask Create a Layer Mask by clicking on the *Add layer mask* button and make sure that your *Foreground color* is set to *Black*. Use the *Brush Tool* on the Layer Mask to paint over any areas where you have coloured outside of the lines, including the eyes and mouth.

5 Paint in hair colour Click on *Create a new layer* again in the Layers palette and choose a *Foreground color* to suit your subject's hair. Once again, use the *Brush Tool* to paint the hair colour onto your image, again not worrying too much about going outside of the edges.

6 Change Blend Mode In the Layers palette, change the *Blend Mode* of this layer. The Blend Mode will depend on the colour of your subject's hair. It's worth trying both *Color* and *Soft Light* to see which produces the nicest effect, again adjusting *Opacity* if needed.

7 Add a Layer Mask Add a *Layer Mask* to the same layer and brush out any areas of overspill. Repeat these steps for each section of colour, starting on a new layer each time and experimenting with the *Blend Mode* and *Opacity* for each layer until you're happy with the finish.

8 Experiment with colour Don't be afraid to have fun with the colours that you choose. Obviously certain things have to be the correct colour to look right, but there's no reason why you can't spice things up by experimenting with different background or clothing colours.

Turn pictures into a sketch

Eager to try artistic effects on your images, but not sure how? Follow this tutorial to see your photograph transform into a detailed drawing

Luke Marsh: Post-production of photographs needn't be limited to a clean-up or colour and tonal adjustments. CS and Elements have a host of filters that can use the information in the image to convert the picture into different styles, even mediums, for creative effect. For instance, unless you're talented with a pencil, chances are you wouldn't be able to create a detailed sketch of this standard from a photograph without the help of Photoshop. Try it for yourself with a portrait that has a simple, blurred background so as not to distract from the subject and sketch detailing.

Workflow tools

☑ **THE FILTER GALLERY**

If you go to *Filter>Filter Gallery…* you'll be presented with many creative filters. The filters are categorised into sections such as Artistic, Distort, Sketch and Texture, and by clicking on the section folders, you can access the filters. Click on a filter icon and you are presented with a large preview of your image along with a set of controls allowing you to fine-tune the filter's effect. Take time to experiment with them all.

Original

1 Desaturate The first thing to do is desaturate the image. Go to *Image>Adjustments>Hue/Saturation* and move the *Saturation* slider to *-100%*. With the *Foreground* and *Background colors* set to *Black* and *White*, go to *Select>All*. Now go to *Edit>Cut* then *Edit>Paste* to remove the image from the background and paste onto a new layer.

2 Apply Graphic Pen Create a duplicate from the original image by going to *Layer>Duplicate Layer* and name the layer 'Graphic Pen'. Next, go to *Filter>Sketch>Graphic Pen…* and enter the *Stroke Length* as *15* and *Light/Dark Balance* as *60*, then set the *Direction* to *Left Diagonal*, and click *OK*. Change the layer's *Blend Mode* to *Multiply* and the layer's *Opacity* to *40%*.

3 Find the edges Duplicate the original image layer once more, this time naming the layer 'Find Edges', then drag the layer above the 'Graphic Pen' layer in the Layers palette. Next, go to *Filter>Stylize>Find Edges* to recreate the appearance of a pencil outline. As before, change the layer's *Blend Mode* to *Multiply* and reduce the *Opacity*, this time to *70%*.

4 Add pencil strokes To create drastic pencil strokes, first create a new layer by going to *Layer>New>Layer…*, naming the layer 'Pencil Strokes' and moving this new layer to the top of the Layers palette. Now go to *Edit>Fill…* and change *Use* to *Black* and click *OK*. Finally, add some noise with *Filter>Noise>Add noise*, entering the maximum value and ensuring *Monochromatic* is ticked.

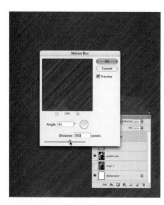

5 Refine the strokes Open *Image>Adjustments>Levels…* and adjust the black and white sliders until the preview shows white dots on solid black. Next, go to *Filter>Blur>Motion Blur…* and change the *Angle* to *45°* and the *Distance* to around *300* pixels and click *OK*. Finally, change the layer's *Blend Mode* to *Overlay* and reduce the *Opacity* to *85%*.

6 Boost the contrast To increase the image's overall contrast without losing any sketch detailing, drag the remaining original image layer to the top of the Layers palette. Change the layer *Blend Mode* to *Overlay* and you'll see a vast improvement in contrast. The effect will appear harsh, so adjust the *Opacity* slider to between *40-50%* to reduce its strength.

7 Add a Layer Mask The problem at this stage is that the sketch is almost too perfect. Rectify this by spending some time hand-painting areas on a Layer Mask, making the image seem more like it's been drawn. The bulk of the image detail is stored on the 'Graphic Pen' layer, so click the layer and go to *Layer>New>Layer Mask>Reveal All* to add the Layer Mask.

8 Hide detail Select the *Brush Tool* and load the *Dry Media Brushes* set from the Brushes panel. Ensuring the *Foreground color* is *Black*, work around the edges, often reducing the *Opacity* slider of the brush to around *50%* for a more subtle effect. I also work on the jacket area and eyes, changing the brush colour back to White if I need to restore any areas.

Final image
Don't be too rigid
with this technique:
imperfections make
the sketch look
more realistic.

Give your favourite portrait a 1950s-style makeover!

Continue your creative streak after you've taken a great portrait and style yourself a piece of retro wall art using this Pop-ular Photoshop technique

Caroline Wilkinson: When someone says Andy Warhol, probably one of the first images to pop into your head is a colourful montage of Marilyn Monroe or a Campbell's soup can. Warhol is one of the most recognised artists of the 1950's pop-art movement and we're still replicating his style 60 years later, with a lot more ease since the introduction of Photoshop. When it comes to picking an image for a Photoshopped pop-art image, it's best to choose a shot with good contrast because you'll be, in effect, using the shadows as a black outline for your colours. Without good shadow detail to define the face, your subject may look like they're without a nose or mouth. If you're unsure, check the image by turning it black & white and then clicking **Image>Adjustment>Threshold** to play with the slider to see if enough detail is retained. You should also try to pick an image with a background that contrasts with the subject to make it easier to extract with the Magic Wand Tool. Some shots work better than others, but it's a case of trial and error. So what are you waiting for? Give your shots a new lease of life with this graphic Photoshop technique.

Be a wand wizard!
If you struggle selecting the whole background, increase or decrease the **Tolerance** level of your wand slightly and hold **Shift** while making multiple selections.

1 Create new layers Open the image and duplicate it (*Layer>Duplicate Layer*). Now go to *Layer>New Adjustment Layer> Solid Color...* and pick the colour you want your background to be. Next, click and drag this layer between the two image layers and click the top layer.

2 Colour the background Use the *Magic Wand Tool* to select the background and press the *backspace* key to reveal the coloured layer beneath. Go to *Select>Deselect*, then *Image>Adjustments> Desaturate* and then *Image>Adjustments> Threshold*, adjusting the slider to retain facial details.

3 Add blur Add a touch of blur by going to *Filter>Blur> Gaussian Blur* and setting the slider to *1px*. Drag the top layer onto the *Add new layer* icon to duplicate. Select the *Paint Bucket Tool* and press the *X* key to select *White*, then click on the face. (*X* changes the Foreground color from Black to White).

4 Colour the skin Set the top layer's *Blend Mode* to *Multiply* so it interacts with the layer beneath, click on the next layer and then add a *Solid Color* adjustment layer, this time picking a colour for the skin. Select the *Paint Bucket Tool*, press *X*, and fill the layer with *Black* to mask the colour.

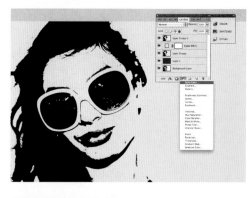

5 Link the layers Hold *Alt* and click between the second and third layer. Now select the *Brush Tool* and press *X* to choose *White* as the *Foreground color* and paint over the skin area. Next, using *Solid Color* adjustment layers, add as many extra colours as you need, clipping each one to the layer below it.

6 Crop the image Select the *Crop Tool* and hold down *Shift* while dragging from the top left to bottom right to create a square image. Move the square until you're happy with the crop. Double-click to complete. Select all layers except the Background layer by holding *Shift* and clicking on each layer.

7 Create the series Press *Cmd+T* to enter Free Transform. In the options bar at the top, change the *Width* and *Height* to *50%*, and move the image to the top left of the picture. Select the *Move Tool*, hold *Alt*, drag the shot to the top right, then copy the image three times and position the boxes.

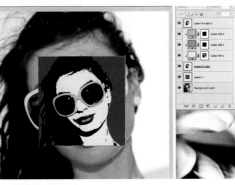

8 Change colours To change the background colours, scroll down the Layers palette to select the right layer, pick a colour and click on the selected layer with the *Paint Bucket Tool*. For other features you want to change the colour of, double-click on that layer's coloured box for the colour picker.

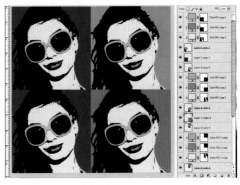

Turn pictures into paintings

Want to make your images fit for an art gallery? Follow this tutorial to see your picture transform into a stunning watercolour masterpiece…

Luke Marsh: Photoshop has a plethora of filters and artistic presets that most of us have probably dabbled with out of curiosity. Few of us, though, know how to get the best out of these filters and quite often get deterred by disappointing results. Clicking on *Filter>Artistic>Watercolor...* is usually the first and only step most people take when trying to convert one of their photographs into a pseudo painting, and while this can create an acceptable finish, combining it with other artistic filters can produce more convincing images that might have people questioning whether the image is indeed a photograph or a print of a painting. Here we show you how to do this using four different effects and the best way of applying the Watercolor filter. You might want to look for further brushes online – see the panel (right) to find out how to download some for free.

Workflow tools

✓ BRUSH DOWNLOADS

If after investigating Photoshop's pre-installed brushes you feel there's nothing that quite works, search online for brush sets to download. Sites like www.brusheezy.com and www.myphotoshopbrushes.com have loads of categorised brush sets that are free to download for personal use. Downloading a set will give you a .abr file – to use it, simply place this file into the Photoshop brushes folder: *User>Library>Application Support>Adobe>Adobe Photoshop>Presets>Brushes* (Mac), or *C:\>Program Files>Adobe>Photoshop> Presets>Brushes* (PC). Open Photoshop and select your new brush sets via *Windows> Brush Panel* and you're ready to begin painting.

Original

ADAM BURTON

1 Prepare the layers Open your chosen image and go to *Select>All* and then *Edit>Cut*, followed by *Edit>Paste* to cut the entire image area from the background, placing it on its own layer. Next, go to *Layer>New>Group...*, creating a folder icon in the Layers palette. Drag the image layer into this folder. A Layer Mask will be added to this group later on, allowing all layers within it to be edited as one. Now click the *Background layer* and go to *Layer>New>Layer via Copy*, creating a layer above the background but below the group.

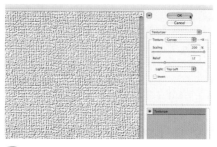

2 Add texture On the background copy layer, go to *Filter>Texture>Texturizer...* and in the preview window, select *Canvas* as the *Texture*, increase *Scaling* to maximum value (*200%*), set *Relief* to between *10* and *15*, and *Light* to *Top Left*, then click *OK*. Now change the *Opacity* of the layer to around *50%*. Click on the image layer in the group folder and go to *Layer>Duplicate Layer*, creating a duplicate of the layer above it. Repeat this once more so there are three identical image layers within the group folder.

3 Apply pencil outline Click on the top layer in the folder to activate it. Go to *Filter>Stylize>Find Edges*. Next, go to *Image>Adjustments>Hue/Saturation* and move the *Saturation* slider to *-100* to remove the colour so that the edges in the image look like they've been drawn by pencil. Finally, change the layer *Blend Mode* to *Multiply* and reduce the *Opacity* to *50-60%*. Once complete, hide the layer by clicking on the *eye* icon next to the layer's thumbnail in the Layers palette.

Work of art!
With a few easy steps, people will think you're as good a painter as you are a photographer.

4 Add the watercolour The watercolour effect is built up from the other two layers in the group folder. First, click on the middle layer and go to *Filter>Artistic>Watercolor...* and enter *Brush Detail* as *7*, *Shadow Intensity* as *0* and *Texture* as *1*. Change the layer *Blend Mode* to *Overlay* and reduce the *Opacity* to *50%*, then hide the layer. Click on the bottom layer and go to *Filter>Brush Strokes>Accented Edges...* and enter *Edge Width* as *2*, *Edge Brightness* as *15* and *Smoothness* as *8*. Finally, change the layer *Opacity* to *80%*.

5 Edit the effect Make all three layers visible by clicking the *eye* icons to see the complete watercolour effect. To give the impression that this is a real painting on canvas, you will need to add a hand-brushed border. To do this, first click on the *folder* icon and go to *Layer>Layer Mask>Reveal All*. Applying a Layer Mask to the group rather than individual layers allows all the layers to be edited at once. Change the group *Blend Mode* to *Multiply* and its *Opacity* to *90%*, allowing the canvas texture to show through.

6 Create an art border With the Layer Mask selected, paint over the image with the *Brush Tool*. Choose from the default brushes or download artistic brushes (see panel) – for this step-by-step I downloaded a set of free watercolour brushes. Change the brush *Color* to *Black*, set an appropriate *Size*, then work around the edge of the image, using artistic licence, to build up the border. Whenever you think you've overdone it, simply change the brush colour to *White* and work over the area to restore the detail.

Create a miniature scene

Sometimes you want to have a bit of fun with your pictures and you'll soon have your friends scratching their heads with this illusion

Luke Marsh: The introduction of the Lensbaby optic gave miniaturisation – once the preserve of pros with big budgets – a well-earned comeback in recent years. And where there's a popular in-camera technique, it's never long before we try to replicate it in Photoshop. This digital technique is a simple combination of Photoshop's Lens Blur filter and a Layer Mask applied to a portion of the image. The best images to use are those our brains process as normal scale in terms of large and small subjects next to one another, such as people next to buildings, a house dwarfed by mountains or in this case boats moored in a harbour. So how does it work? Well, it's all to do with how we perceive depth-of-field. When we see scenes from a distance, our eyes keep the entire scene in focus. However, if we try to focus on a subject a very short distance in front of us, it's impossible to keep the scene behind it sharp. What the blur is doing is mimicking this phenomenon and by doing so is fooling the brain into thinking that the boats are very close, but because we can also see all the boats, the brain's assumption is that they must be very small, like a toy set. Confused? I know I am!

Original

HOT KEY Q

Q = Quick Mask
Quick Mask mode is activated by pressing *Q*. It allows you to highlight areas of an image that will then become marquee selections once you exit the mode by pressing *Q* again. The Brush is the suggested tool for this mode, as by using varying sizes and hardness you can achieve very accurate selections.

1 Create a duplicate layer With the file open, go *Layer>Duplicate Layer...* to create a copy. Add a Layer Mask by going to *Layer>Layer Mask...>Hide All*. The Layer Mask icon in the Layers palette (circled) should appear black. Once edited this allows for blurring of the top layer while viewing a portion of the original beneath.

2 Make a Reflected Gradient Select the *Gradient Tool* and change the gradient type to *Reflected* by clicking on the fourth icon along in the Options bar (circled). Now press the *Q* key (see panel) to change to *Quick Mask* mode. When active, the words 'Quick Mask' appear at the end of the image file name at the top of the window.

3 Create a Quick Mask While holding the *Shift* key to ensure a straight line, draw a gradient at the bottom of the image by dragging up or down, and letting go once finished. It may take a few attempts to highlight the desired area, so you may need to go to *Edit>Undo* (or *Cmd + Z*) to undo the masked area and then try again.

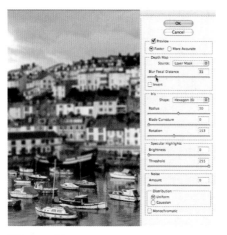

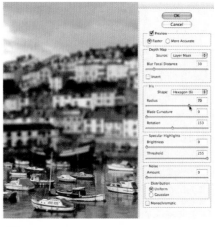

4 Edit the Layer Mask With the Quick Mask created, press *Q* again to leave this mode – you will now have a marquee selection. To add this selection to the Layer Mask, make sure the Layer Mask thumbnail is selected (circled). Then go to *Edit>Fill...*, select *White* and click *OK*. To remove the marquee selection go to *Edit>Deselect*.

5 Lens Blur Click back on to the image thumbnail and go to *Filter>Blur>Lens Blur...* In the window that opens first, ensure the *Depth Map Source* is set to *Layer Mask* then change the *Blur Focal Distance* to around *30*. When using a picture where the focal point is positioned differently, you will need to adjust this figure.

6 Increase the blur Finally, to improve the miniature effect, increase the blur amount by adjusting the *Radius*. You'll need to use quite a lot of blur – no less than 60 – but the trick is to use the optimum amount for your specific image without overdoing the effect. It might take a bit of trial and error to get it right.

Final image
We've achieved a fantastic tilt & shift effect with just a few relatively simple clicks and tweaks in Photoshop.

Create a caricature

You don't always have to be reserved with your retouching – have a bit of fun and use the Liquify filter to exaggerate features for comic effect

Caroline Wilkinson: Sometimes using the Liquify filter to create bigger eyes, lips or muscles can flatter a subject, but if taken to the extreme this filter can distort a person beyond recognition. Normally we'd advocate making many small adjustments to avoid this and to ensure natural and subtle results by slowly building up the effect – but where's the fun in that?

For this tutorial, enlarge that brush Size, increase its Rate and boost that Pressure for some uninhibited fun and to distort a portrait into a caricature. Even though you'll be exaggerating your subject's key features, there should still be an easily identifiable visual likeness, so try to build on what's already there. For instance, if they have big eyes, make them bigger. If they have a large nose, exaggerate it even more. One of the distinguishing features of a caricature is the distortion of perspective: making the head much bigger than the body or the forehead a lot wider than their tapered chin, or vice versa, for instance. Have a go with your family photos and why not send us your funniest faces?

TOP TIP

Reconstruct
If you want to undo your distortions, you can click *Restore All* in the *Reconstruct Options* panel to revert the image back to its original state. However, if you wish to only reconstruct a part of your image, select the *Reconstruct Tool* in the toolbar and click on the area you want to restore. If you do use this tool, make sure the *Reconstruct Mode* (in the Options panel) is set to *Revert* so the image can backstep to its original state.

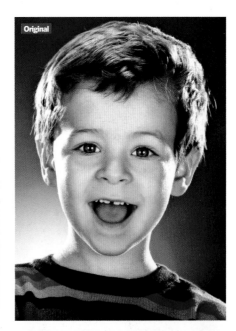
Original

1 Create a duplicate layer Open the image in Photoshop and go *Layer>Duplicate Layer*, so you're working on a copy. Now click *Filter>Liquify* to load the layer into the Liquify filter. The dialogue box opens with a preview image in the centre and the toolbar to the left with the options bar to the right. Zoom in to the picture so it fills the preview window to make adjustments easier.

2 Inflate the eyes A good place to start distorting is the eyes. Select the *Bloat Tool* and a brush *Size* that's as big as the eye socket. Place the cursor in the centre of the pupil, then click and hold to see the eye inflate. If the effect is too fast or too heavy, reduce the brush *Rate* or increase it if it's not fast enough. For the best effect, it's important to click in one area, then drag the tool.

3 Bloat the forehead To refine the shape of the eye, reduce the brush *Size* and click around the edge of the eye to bloat that, too. If the pupil changes shape, simply click in the centre again. Use the *Pucker Tool* to reduce the overall effect. While you've got the *Bloat Tool* selected, increase the brush *Size* so it's proportional with the forehead and click to expand this area.

4 Make a mask Reduce the brush *Size* again and puff out the cheeks a little with the *Bloat Tool*. To target the teeth, but not the lips, select the *Freeze Mask Tool* and click the *Show Mask* icon in the Options panel. Adjust the brush *Size* and paint over the areas you don't want to be affected. If you do too much, switch to the *Thaw Mask Tool* and simply erase what you don't need.

5 Enlarge the teeth Now with the *Forward Warp Tool* set to a brush no bigger than the tooth, click and drag the bottom of the tooth down to enlarge it without affecting the lip. When you're done, use the *Thaw Mask Tool* to erase the mask. Now use the *Forward Warp Tool* to subtly extend the smile if you need to or switch to the *Bloat Tool* to puff up the lips, nose and ears.

6 Reshape the face Now use the *Forward Warp Tool* (set to a large brush of *300-600*, with a medium *Pressure* of *50* and a *Rate* of *26*), to distort the face. To narrow the chin, click on the jawline and drag it in to narrow the face. To elongate the chin, click and drag downwards. You can also use the same technique to stretch the neck by pushing down the shoulders.

Final image
This is an easy and enjoyable technique to try on your children's photographs or a family portrait. Give it a go!

Create a rainy-day portrait

Today we forecast a heavy downpour! Give your images the illusion of rain with a few tweaks using Noise and Motion Blur…

Luke Marsh: For most photographers, shooting in the rain isn't their favourite pastime, but it can add a different dimension to your pictures. So how can you create the appearance of rain without having to actually get you or your camera gear wet? Easy, follow this technique!

Its success lies in trying to make the scene look authentic, so if your starting image is of a street scene, make sure it was taken just after it's rained, when the ground is still wet. Similarly, have your subject/s hold an umbrella for the same reasons – if it's pouring with rain, they'd be soaking wet without one. An umbrella is the perfect cover-up, quite literally.

Original

ISTOCK PHOTO

Secrets unlocked

☑ LET IT SNOW, LET IT SNOW!

You can also adapt this rain technique to create a great snow effect! In step four, when using Motion Blur, reduce the **Distance** down to less than **10** pixels to give the appearance of drifting snow, as opposed to heavy rain. Also, having different-sized flakes adds extra dimension to the scene, so go to **Layer>New>Layer via Copy** to duplicate the layer. Then **Edit>Transform>Scale** to increase the size of the new snow layer by holding **Shift** and dragging a corner widget.

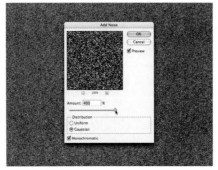

1 Open your image Create a new layer above the original by going to **Layer>New Layer...** and clicking **OK** in the pop-up window. To be able to affect this layer, you need to put content into it. For this, go to **Edit>Fill...** and, under Contents, change **Use** to **Black** and ensure **Mode** is **Normal** and **Opacity** is **100** under the Blending Options.

2 Add some noise Now add noise to the new black layer by going to **Filter>Noise>Add noise...**. Select **Gaussian** under **Distribution**, and ensure that **Monochromatic** is ticked. The **Amount** of noise you need to enter will depend on the image's resolution. For large files, you will need to enter the maximum amount of **400%**.

3 Scale the noise Even though the maximum amount of noise was used, the noise 'dots' need to be bigger (the higher the image resolution and size, the more this will be the case). Go to **Edit>Transform>Scale**, enter **400%** in the horizontal scale field and click the **link** icon to scale in proportion. Double-click to apply.

4 Create raindrops Now change the noise layer's *Blend Mode* to *Screen*, making the image beneath visible. The noise needs editing to create fine raindrops, so go to *Image> Adjustments>Levels...* and drag the *black slider* all the way to the right, making the drops smaller and allowing a better interaction with the image.

5 Blur the raindrops Use *Filter>Blur>Motion Blur...* to add the effect of moving rain. In the control panel, enter an *Angle* that suits your particular image. Here, 60° was used to reflect the position the little girl holds her umbrella. Then enter a *Distance* that gives intermittent streaks rather than solid lines running across the image.

6 Perfect the storm The final tweaks are done using Levels (*Image>Adjustments> Levels...*). Move the *black* and white sliders to change the rain's appearance depending on your image. The black slider reduces the appearance of rain from sheets to drizzle, whereas the white slider improves the contrast of the rain.

Create a misty morning

Using the Gradient Tool and a few other little Photoshop tricks, you can give your images an eerie wintery feel that's full of atmosphere

Original

Luke Marsh: Mist is one of those elusive elements that rarely appears when you want it to but when it does it can transform the atmosphere of your landscapes. Now, this step-by-step is no substitute for the real thing, but it can be used to improve your current landscape images or to occasionally relieve you of having to wake early on a winter morning to search for natural mist.

Deep valleys and rolling hills make beautiful scenes for misty landscapes, as do frost-bitten fields. Refer to some example images before you try this technique just to see how mist naturally acts in different situations. Mist tends to look gradually heavier the further it is away from you, which is why you'll notice we handle the image treatment in sections: background, middle-distance and foreground, with each one having a different intensity of mist.

HOT KEY

Set Foreground & Background Color When using Layer Masks or the Gradient Tool, press the *X* key to change between the Foreground and Background Color, which by default should be set to Black and White.

1 Add a gradient Use *Layer>New>Layer...* to create a layer above the original. Select the *Gradient Tool* and ensure it's set to *Linear gradient* in the Options bar, and that the *Foreground color* is set to *White* and the *Background color* to *Black*, as shown. Click and hold, then drag from the top of the image to just under the horizon to create the background layer of mist.

2 Reveal the tree In reality, the mist would be behind the tree. To give it this appearance, first add a *Layer Mask* by clicking the icon in the Layers palette (circled). Next, select the *Brush Tool*, set to *Black* and an appropriate *Size*, and begin to work over the tree, removing the mist. If you go too far, you can change the brush colour to *White* and paint over the area to bring the detail back.

3 Focus on the middle-distance To add fog to the middle-distance, create another new layer via *Layer>New>Layer...* Use the *Gradient Tool* with the same settings, and draw a line from the top to the bottom of the image and release to create an even gradient across the image. Reduce the *Opacity* slider by changing the amount to *50%* in the Layers palette (circled).

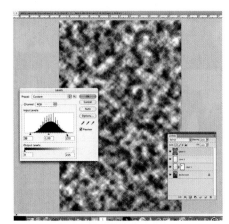

4 Add foreground mist To create eerie foreground mist, again create a new layer (*Layer>New>Layer...*), then go to *Filter>Render> Clouds* to fill the layer with a textured cloud effect. Use *Image>Adjustments>Levels...* and the black and white sliders to boost the contrast on the image. Finally, change the layer's *Blend Mode* to *Screen* to make the layers interact.

5 Adjust perspective To add perspective to the clouded mist, go to *Edit>Free Transform> Scale* and reduce down to the foreground area by dragging the top-centre tab. Before applying, change the transform to *Perspective* and drag one of the bottom corner tabs outside the pasteboard until you're happy. You may need to zoom out to move the tabs out far enough, as shown here.

6 Tweak colour & contrast Create two Adjustment Layers by selecting the icon at the bottom of the Layers palette (circled). First, create a *Hue/Saturation* adjustment layer and use the *Saturation* slider to desaturate the colours slightly. Finally, create a *Brightness/Contrast* adjustment layer to boost the contrast sufficiently to enhance the appearance of diffused misty light.

Final image
A few simple steps are all it
takes to add a touch of mist
to your landscape images.

Create 'golden hour' light

A balmy summer's evening can give a supremely flattering glow to your subject. Recreate the look using Curves and the Burn Tool…

Luke Marsh: There's nothing quite like a glorious summer sunset to add ambience and colour to your portrait images. However, capturing such a backlit effect can be technically challenging with tricky metering and flare posing problems, but with this simple step-by-step you can transform daytime portraits with minimal effort.

You can try this technique on any outdoor portrait, but the effect will be more dramatic the cooler the original image tones are. You rarely see clouds when there's a burning sunset so, if you can, pick an image with a generous expanse of clear blue sky in a summery location such as a flower-filled field or one with plenty of lush greenery. An image with shallow depth-of-field can also enhance the final hazy warmth of the image, though it's not essential.

Getting the Photoshop effect correct relies on you working well with Layer Masks, but the beauty of them is that they're fully editable so you can refine and retry the technique without damaging your original image. Use Black paint and a soft brush on a Layer Mask to hide effects and White paint to reveal them again, altering the Opacity for better control.

QUICK FIND

Layer Masks Click the Add *Layer Mask icon* at the bottom of the Layers palette. A thumbnail appears on the active layer in the palette.

Adjustment Layers Click and hold on the *New Adjustment Layer* icon at the bottom of the Layers palette, then scroll down to select the adjustment .

Original

1 Create the sun First, add the sun. To do this, create a duplicate of the original image: go to *Layer>New>Layer via Copy*, then open *Filter>Render>Lens Flare...* Select *105mm Prime* from *Lens Type* and position the small cross hairs on the thumbnail preview. Finally, enter an appropriate *Brightness* amount for the image.

2 Improve the face The flare strength means the subject's face appears very burnt out. To solve this, add a *Layer Mask* by clicking the icon in the Layers palette. Select a soft-edged brush, set to *Black*, with an *Opacity* of around *20%*, and paint over the subject to reduce the effects of the flare, without removing it completely.

3 Sunset gradient In the toolbar, make sure the *Background Color* is *White*, then click on the *Foreground Color* icon. In the Color Picker, change to a sunset colour. Now click on the *Add new adjustment layer* icon in the Layers palette and select *Gradient...* Set *Style* to *Linear* and tick *Reverse*, so the gradient runs from top to bottom.

Final image
Give your images the Midas touch by adding a gorgeous sunset to your shots.

4 Tweak the gradient Change the *Blend Mode* to *Color*. To reduce the colour tint on the subject, use a *Layer Mask*, as in step two. A Gradient adjustment layer has a Layer Mask by default, so click on it in the Layers palette, select a medium soft-edged brush, set to *Black*, with *Opacity* at *20%*, and begin work on the subject.

5 Use Curves Click the *Add new adjustment layer* icon and choose *Curves...* Now you can create an 'S' curve or choose *Strong Contrast* from the *Preset* menu and click *OK*. The effect can be harsh on the subject's face, so add a *Layer Mask* and reduce the effects by using the *Brush Tool* set to *Black*, as in the previous step.

6 Burn the foreground To finish, click on the duplicate image layer that holds the flare, ensuring the image thumbnail is active and not the Layer Mask. Select the *Burn Tool* and, using a large soft-edged brush with *Opacity* set to about *20%*, begin to work around the foreground of the image to darken it off, adding depth to the image.

Create a ten-stop ND effect

Neutral Density filters are brilliant, but require a level of dedication to get consistently great results. Here's a technique for those of you who want to trial the effect or don't have the time to attempt the real thing

Luke Marsh: For any of you who aren't already aware, the ten-stop ND filter is amazing! By significantly lengthening a camera's exposure, the filter allows the camera to capture motion so clouds are rendered as streaks and water becomes a fine mist – it's truly magnificent, but it takes skill and patience to perfect. As great as this in-camera technique is, often the key to its success is the location, and with exposure times often more than an hour long, it demands extreme dedication and time – if you're anything like me, those are two things I can't always spare in my hectic schedule.

There is, however, a shortcut to getting a very similar effect using Photoshop's Blur filters, and while it may not be one for the photo-purist, it can produce a very convincing comparison when combined with the right kind of image. Feel free to experiment on any image, but it's usually coastal scenes that produce the most dramatic results. For further inspiration of what images might work, it's worth looking at contributor Lee Frost's motion studies project (www.leefrost.co.uk), taken with an actual ten-stop ND filter.

HOW TO USE...

Layer Masks
A Layer Mask allows you to hide detail from the layer it's applied to, revealing the image beneath, without erasing it. When the Layer Mask is selected, simply add the colour *Black* to the mask to hide image detail and change to the colour white to restore the detail. Use the *X* key to quickly switch between the colours.

Original

1 Create duplicate layers First, create a duplicate layer from the Background layer by going to *Layer>Duplicate Layer...*, naming the layer accordingly – here, it's called 'Water Blur'. Then click on the *Add layer mask* icon at the bottom of the Layers palette to add a Layer Mask. Repeat this process to create an additional duplicate layer – this one was named 'Sky Blur'.

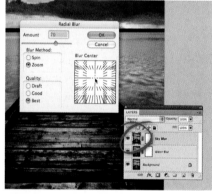

2 Apply Radial Blur On the sky layer, ensure the image thumbnail is selected (circled), then go to *Filter>Blur>Radial Blur...* In the Radial Blur window, make sure that the *Blur Method* is *Zoom* and *Quality* is set to *Best*. Next, enter a large *Amount* – no less than 50 – and move the Blur Center to an area where the horizon would roughly be positioned on the image, and click *OK*.

3 Hide foreground blur The Radial Blur should only affect the sky portion of this layer, so click on the *Layer Mask* thumbnail in the Layers palette (circled) and, with the *Brush Tool* set to a large soft-edged brush and *Black* colour, paint across the foreground area to hide the blur across the water and jetty. Switch to a smaller brush when working near the horizon.

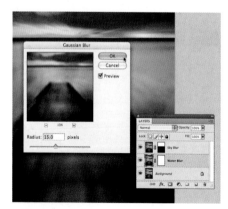

4 Blur the water Switch to the water layer by clicking on it. Add a *Radial Blur zoom blur*, with all the settings as in step two, but reducing the *Amount* down by half, just to make the cloud reflections more realistic. Then go to *Filter>Blur> Gaussian Blur...*, setting the amount to no more than *15* pixels. This adds a hazy sheen to water, common with many long-exposure images.

5 Reveal the jetty Now edit the Layer Mask to reveal the jetty. First, click on the *Layer Mask* thumbnail (circled), then select the *Polygonal Lasso Tool* and draw a selection around the edge of the jetty. Once complete, go to *Select>Modify> Feather...* and add a value of *1* pixel to avoid a harsh edge to the selection. Now take the *Brush Tool*, still set to *Black*, and paint over the selection.

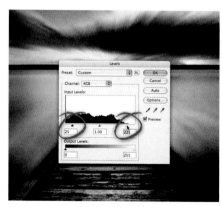

6 Convert to mono To turn the image mono, go to *Image>Adjustments>Black & White...* and click *OK* to use the default settings. Conversions from colour to mono often leave an image looking a little flat, so use *Image>Adjustments>Levels...* to add contrast. Use the black point and white point sliders (circled) to boost the blacks and whites respectively, taking care not to burn out any detail.

Final image
With just a few steps, you could add this beautiful atmospheric effect to your landscape images.

Give your sunset a striking silhouette

Follow this step-by-step to see how using a pseudo silhouette for a focal point can improve your pictures

Caroline Wilkinson: When shooting sunsets, there's very little that you can control. While you can prepare for a sudden glow by scouting out locations beforehand, sometimes the location you end up with isn't as good as the light it receives and a compromise has to be made. While foreground interest and lead-in lines are strong compositional tools, a focal point is paramount. If you struggle to find the perfect spot, you could add composite elements from different images to create a focal point. Most backlit subjects will be silhouetted, so these seem the most obvious addition. Here, the focal point became a silhouetted tree at the end of the path.

1 Open your tree image It can be tricky to extract a tree with all its small details and erratic edges, but this process makes it simple. Open your Layers palette and then the *Channels* palette, accessible via the *Window* menu, then pick the channel that shows the most contrast between the tree and background. For this image, it's the Blue channel.

2 White out areas Duplicate the *Blue* channel so you're not working on the original channel by clicking and dragging it down to the *Create new Channel* icon at the bottom of the palette. If there are areas around the tree that aren't white, select the *Brush Tool* with a soft edge and *100% Opacity*, then use *White* paint to fill in the areas.

3 Adjust the Levels Still with the new copy layer selected, go to *Image>Adjustments>Levels*. Adjust the exposure by moving the black and white sliders slowly inwards to bleach the background and darken the tree. Now, click on the *Load Channel as a selection* button at the bottom of the palette, and then *Select>Inverse* to select the tree and *Edit>Copy* to copy the tree.

4 Edit the landscape Next, open your landscape image in Photoshop and make any necessary adjustments. For this one, we wanted to enhance the colour of the sunset so applied a Hue/Saturation adjustment layer (*Layer>New Adjustment Layer>Hue/Saturation*) to intensify the colour and to add more warmth. You might find you need a contrast or exposure adjustment.

5 Apply the tree With the Background layer selected, go to *Edit>Paste* to add the tree to the image. It should be visible as a new layer above the Background layer. With the *Move Tool* selected and with the tree layer active, hold down *Shift* while you adjust the corners of the bounding box to scale the image appropriately and proportionally.

6 Link layers Use the *Move Tool* to position the tree in place. Change the layer's *Blend Mode* to *Multiply*. Now adjust the exposure to enhance the silhouette: apply a *Levels* adjustment layer, but before you make any changes, press *Alt* and hover over the line between the layers in the Layers palette until two circles appear. Click to link the layers together.

Final image
Notice how adding a focal point keeps your eye within the picture for longer, compared to the original.

7 Edit the exposure By linking the layers together, it means any changes you make to the *Levels* layer only affect the layer directly below it. Now move the black and grey triangle sliders to the right until you're happy with the result. Click *OK*. Now add a *Layer Mask* to the tree layer, and use the *Brush Tool* and *Black* paint to edit the bottom of the tree trunk.

8 Select the ground Because the tree is silhouetted and the foreground looks quite bright in comparison, it looks a little odd at the moment. Click on the *Background layer* and then use the *Rectangular Marquee Tool* to select the ground below the horizon. Set the *Feather* (in the Options bar) to *100px* to soften the edges of the selection.

9 Adjust the lighting With the selection still active, apply a *Levels* adjustment layer and then move the black triangle inwards to darken the shadows. Do the same with the grey triangle to darken the mid-tones until the foreground looks as if it balances with the tree's exposure. Save the image as a .PSD file, then merge the layers (*Layers>Flatten Image*) and save as a JPEG.

Turn day into night

Transform daytime scenes into interesting night shots with glowing street lamps, mysterious shadows and transitions from light to dark

Jordan Butters: Have you ever taken a photograph and wished that you had returned after dark to shoot it again? Fear not – you can transform an image from day to night by manipulating light and shadow in Photoshop.

This technique works best with images taken on overcast days, as the natural shadows are softer and less pronounced and therefore require less work to alter and manipulate. It also helps to include visible light sources in the shot – items such as street lamps and windows; the scene will appear more believable if the viewer can see where the light is coming from. The more objects you have in a scene that the light could fall on, the more complex and difficult this technique will be to achieve. For instance, the trees in this image required considerable time to be spent brushing each branch with light, being careful not to affect the dark areas behind them. To make it easier, pick a clear street scene.

Original

TOP TIP...

Casting shadows
Pay attention to any obstacles the light would hit and how the shadows would be cast if the lighting were real. Also consider the direction of surfaces affected by the light and how much illumination they would receive. The human eye is very good at spotting things that don't look quite right, so any areas lit incorrectly may immediately stand out.

1 Duplicate your image Create a copy of your Background layer (*Layer>New>Layer via Copy*) and name this new layer 'Dark' by double-clicking on its name in the Layers palette. Click on the eye icon next to your 'Dark' layer to hide it for now. Select the *Background layer* again by clicking on it in the Layers palette.

2 Create the light Click on the *Create new fill or adjustment layer* button and choose *Hue/Saturation* from the drop-down menu. In the Adjustments palette, tick the *Colorize* box and adjust the *Hue* to around *48* to match the warm yellow cast by street lamps. Click on the eye icon box next to the dark layer to reveal it again.

3 Turn off the lights Make sure the 'Dark' layer is selected and create another Adjustment Layer, choosing *Hue/Saturation* and selecting *Colorize* again. This time, change the *Hue* to a dark blue – around *210* worked here. Lower the *Lightness* to *-75* and the *Saturation* to *15*. Click on *Layer>Create Clipping Mask*.

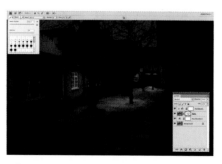

4 Bring back the light With the 'Dark' layer selected, click on the *Add layer mask* button, select the *Brush Tool* and set *Black* as the colour. In the Brush options menu set the *Hardness* to *0%* and lower the *Opacity* to *15%*. Identify the light sources in the image and begin brushing over to introduce the light, gradually building it back up.

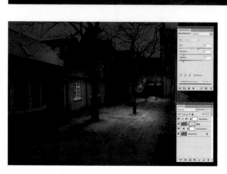

5 Create shadows Press the *X* key to change your *Foreground color* to *White* and using a smaller, harder brush, paint the shadow in where the light wouldn't fall. Select the 'Dark' layer by clicking the thumbnail in the Layers palette and use the *Burn Tool* to further darken shadows such as those cast by the tree closest in our image.

Final image

For extra realism you can add in a moonlit cloudy sky, as we have here. Drop in a stock moon image and set the *Blend Mode* to *Screen*, then all that is left to do is tidy up any overlapping areas using the *Eraser Tool*.

6 **Add a light source** Click on the *Create a new layer* button and select the *Brush Tool* again. Set the *Hardness* to *0%* and the *Opacity* to *20%*. Pick light yellow as your *Foreground color* and click on the light source two or three times to create a glow. The closer the light, the stronger the glow should appear.

7 **Add some exposure** Select *White* as your *Foreground color*, reduce the brush *Size* slightly and click on the light source again three or four times, giving the impression that the bulb is overexposed. Repeat for each light source, reducing the brush *Opacity* the further away the light is from the camera.

8 **Add a filter** Add a *Photo Filter* adjustment layer, as in step two. Applying a filter before saving your final image brings the varying tones closer together for a more realistic finish. We chose to use a Cooling Filter (80), but it's worth trying the other presets as one of the other filters may suit your scene better.

Apply body art

Make your portraits a little more edgy and interesting with this simple step-by-step

Luke Marsh: Tattoos are one of those artistic accessories that you either love or you hate, but whatever camp you sit in, one thing you can't dispute is that they add visual interest and a focal point to a picture. Tattoos are statement pieces, so applying one to a simple image, like this one, allows it to have an unbridled impact. Careful consideration should be given to picking a suitable picture and the placement of the tattoo as you want to enhance, not distract from, the rest of the image.

While the technique for applying the tattoo is quite simple, it'll be much easier if your tattoo image is on a white background first as, if not, you'll need to cleanly select it before placing it on the body, which can be tricky with intricate designs.

1 Combine the files The first thing to do is combine the two files you've chosen. With the tattoo image open, choose *Select>All* then go to *Edit>Copy*, copying the image to the pasteboard. Close the file and open your body image, and go to *Edit>Paste*, placing the tattoo image onto a new layer, above the body image. Now change the layer's *Blend Mode* to *Multiply*, making the white in the tattoo transparent.

2 Resize the tattoo Change the tattoo layer's *Opacity* to around **50%** to give the tattoo a far more subtle and realistic appearance. Now select the *Move Tool* and position the tattoo where you want it on the subject. Go to *Edit>Free Transform* and use the centre and corner tabs to resize the tattoo to suit your subject. Placing the cursor just outside any of the corner tabs will allow you to rotate the tattoo, should you wish to do so.

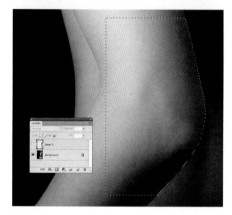

3 Edit the tattoo Limbs that overlap the tattoo can add depth to an image and realism to the effect. To help view the body clearly, hide the tattoo layer by clicking on the eye icon in the Layers palette. Here, the elbow area needs to be selected in order to isolate it from the tattoo. To do this, use the *Polygonal Lasso Tool* to work around the elbow, taking your time to get an accurate selection.

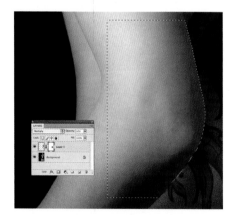

4 Add a Layer Mask Once the selection is made, add a *Feather* to **1** pixel (*Select>Modify>Feather...*). Now create a *Layer Mask* by going to *Layer>Layer Mask>Reveal All*, then go to *Edit>Fill...* and select *Use as Black* and click *OK*. These commands fill the selection with black on the Layer Mask and, subsequently, any of the tattoo underneath the black area is hidden, giving the illusion that the elbow passes in front of it.

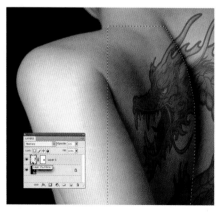

5 Shape the tattoo To edit the tattoo image rather than its Layer Mask, click on the image thumbnail in the Layers palette. The main body contour on this image is the crease in the model's back, so this is where you'd expect to see the most distortion. Using the *Polygonal Lasso Tool*, make a rough selection along the crease and *Feather* the selection to **5** pixels to soften the transition of the Liquify effect you are about to apply.

6 Use Liquify Open the Liquify control panel (*Filter>Liquify...*) where you'll preview the image selection. Ensure *Show Backdrop* is ticked to see the body layer, then select the *Forward Warp Tool* in the top-left corner. Set the *Brush Size* to **250**, then both *Brush Density* and *Brush Pressure* to **50**. Now move the brush down along the crease to distort the tattoo, using *Edit>Undo* if you want to try again. Click *OK* when done.

Final image
Adding a tattoo has given this image more interest as it offers the viewer something to engage with.

How to produce artistic smoke trails

Love taking shots of smoke trails? Then you'll love our new take on the technique. Here's how to do it…

Caroline Wilkinson: Smoke trails are naturally photogenic, but moulding them into a shape as we've done here can create impressive results. This image may look complicated, but the technique is fairly straightforward with only a couple of steps needing to be repeated numerous times to apply the various smoke trails. As a result, you will end up with lots of layers, so we advise you group them together to make it easier on yourself. You also need different types of smoke trails so the effect doesn't look too uniform and all these trails need to be on a black background and desaturated. You're best to do this before starting the tutorial: if your smoke trail is on a white background, open it in Photoshop and go to *Image>Adjustments>Invert*. To desaturate, use *Image>Adjustments>Desaturate*. Also, when manipulating the trails to create the outline of your subject, you'll be using the Transform commands like Scale, Rotate and Warp. To avoid degrading the image quality in the process, make all these edits one after another before committing to any of them. Have fun!

1 Select your subject Use the *Quick Selection Tool* to select the subject. Now go to *Edit>Copy*. Open your background candle image, go to *File>Save As* and rename the image so it's different from the original. Use the *Brush Tool* to paint *Black* over any smoke trails.

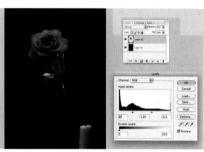

2 Prepare your subject Background layer still selected, click *Edit>Paste* to add the rose to the image. Using the bounding box and the *Move Tool*, rotate and scale the subject to match the angle of the smoke trail you want. Darken the rose using Levels (*Image>Adjustments>Levels*).

3 Apply Glowing Edges Click *Image> Adjustments>Desaturate* to strip the rose of colour and *Filter>Stylize>Glowing Edges*. What settings you use depends on your subject, but we wanted to retain lots of detail while creating a smoke-like outline. Once happy, click *OK*.

4 Add smoke trails Open a trail image in Photoshop. Use the *Lasso Tool* to make a rough selection. Drag the selection onto the main image using the *Move Tool*. Change the new layer's *Blend Mode* to *Screen* so only the trail is visible and its black background merges away.

5 Distort the trails Position lots of small smoke trails around the edge of your subject, using the bounding box to scale and rotate them to suit their placement. Go to *Edit>Transform> Warp* and use the grid to bend and manipulate the trails to fit with the contours of the subject.

6 Organise Repeat steps four and five multiple times using different smoke trails to build the effect. You'll generate lots of layers, so click on *Create new group* at the bottom of the Layers palette and name the folders (ie Petals, Stem and Leaves). Drag your trail layers into these folders.

7 Burn You may find when adding trails that they hide too much of the rose's details, outline or have hard edges. Use the *Burn Tool* set to *Midtones* and an *Exposure* of about *50%* to brush over the edges of the trails. You can do this at any time by clicking on the corresponding layer.

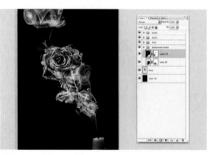

8 Target the background Apply bigger puffs of smoke to link the flower and the candle in the same way you applied the smaller ones. You might need to use a Layer Mask (*Layer>Layer Mask*) with the *Brush Tool* and *Black* paint to edit trails that have covered over your earlier work.

9 Apply a gradient Click on the Rose layer and go to *Layer>Layer Mask*. Select the *Gradient Tool*, making sure *Foreground color* is set to *Black* and the gradient is *Black/White* in the Options bar. Now click and drag from the candle to midway up the rose to blend it with the smoke.

Final image
What do you get when you
cross a rose with a candle?
Smokin' hot shots, that's what!

Add a dispersion effect

Make your subject dissipate using this easy yet impactful technique to manipulate motion and make your action shots far more artistic

Jordan Butters: A fun part of editing and manipulating images is taking a picture beyond the boundaries of reality and this dispersion effect does just that. It allows you to make a moving person or object seem as if they are moving so quickly that they leave trails of colour and particles behind.

An important part of this technique relies on you picking, or shooting, the right type of image. For effective results, pick a picture with motion; it could be as simple as an action shot, someone jumping or hair blowing in the wind. You'll find the selection stage easier if your subject is set against a clean backdrop, too, such as a white wall or blue sky. You'll also need a selection of splat Photoshop brushes, which can be downloaded free from an online brush library, such as www.brusheezy.com.

Workflow tools

☑ **BRUSHES PALETTE**

The Brushes palette window allows you to tweak and manipulate preset brushes to suit your application. From the Brushes palette, you can change the direction and shape of the brush tip, vary the spacing, scatter, shape dynamics and texture, and even apply dual brushes at once. There is a handy preview window at the bottom of the palette for you to see how the adjusted settings affect the brush and its effect.

Original

1 Separate your subject Using the *Quick Selection Tool*, draw around your subject to select the background behind them. If the tool picks out an area you don't want selected, hold down the *Alt* key and go back over the area to deselect. Zoom in and reduce the brush *Size* for detailed areas. Once happy, go *Select>Inverse*.

2 Remove your subject Go to *Edit>Cut* to remove your subject. Select the *Clone Stamp Tool* and hold down the *Alt* key to set your reference point. Begin cloning out the silhouette until you are left with a clean backdrop; it need not be perfect, but the closer the better. Go to *Edit>Paste* to paste your subject onto a new layer.

3 Load the brushes Click on the *Add layer mask* button and select the *Brush Tool*. Go to *Window>Brushes* to bring up the Brushes palette and click on the small menu button at the top right to select *Load Brushes*. Locate the splatter brush set that you have downloaded on your computer and click *Load*.

4 Customise your brushes Scroll down to choose one of the new splatter brushes and select *Brush Tip Shape* on the left. Set the brush size using the slider and the angle of your brush by rotating the compass on the right. The angle of your brush should match the direction that your subject is moving in.

5 Start masking Making sure that your *Foreground color* is set to *Black*, begin clicking to mask areas of your subject, revealing the background behind. Repeat the previous step after each click to change the brush and vary the effect. Once happy with this stage, click on the *Create new layer* button in the Layers palette.

6 Add splats and trails Select the *Brush Tool* and once again go into the Brushes palette. Choose a splatter and set the *Angle* of your brush. Before you apply each splat, use the *Eyedropper Tool* to pick a colour sample from your subject. Select the *Brush Tool* again and apply the splat, starting from the area of colour you selected.

Final image
Keep repeating the final step, changing brush shape, angle and colour before each splat. Try not to place two identical splats near one another or the effect will appear too uniform. Each splat or paint trail should match the colour of the area from which it begins.

Create a comic book story

Present your pictures in a way that you've never seen them before by following this step-by-step to creating your own comic book strip

Luke Marsh: Most young boys – and probably a few bigger boys, too – like comic books, so what better way to present a series of pictures than as a comic book story? Do you have a series of shots taken at one event or trip, or fancy shooting new images with the view to creating a dedicated story? This tutorial will show you how to treat each picture, but the rest is up to you. It could be a narrative comprising numerous pictures, a short three-panel strip or just one image with a humorous or landmark caption to frame on the wall. If you do go to the effort of creating a story, why not have the pictures printed and bound? It would make a great gift or memento. If you have kids, it's a chance to have some fun, too: why not photograph their football skills or, if they're young enough, have them dress up in a superhero outfit for their own Marvel comic.

Original

1 Duplicate layers With the *Foreground Color* set to *Black* and the *Background color* to *White*, select the image area by going *Select>All*. Now go to *Edit>Cut* then *Edit>Paste* to remove the image from the background and paste onto a new layer above the background. Next, create a duplicate of the original image on a separate layer by using *Layer>New>Layer via Copy*, and change this layer's *Blend Mode* to *Darken*.

2 Add Motion Blur Now add some blur to create the appearance of movement. Go to *Filter>Blur>Motion Blur* and change the *Angle* to suit your image, then increase the *Distance* to around *200* pixels and click *OK*. Add a Layer Mask with *Layer>Layer Mask>Reveal All*, and use a medium-sized brush, set to *Black* and with a soft edge, and paint on to the image to remove blur detail, leaving blur around the edge of the subject.

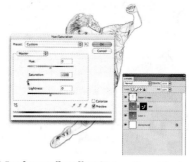

3 Apply pencil outline Click on the original image layer and duplicate it again, then move this layer to the top of the Layers palette. Go to *Filter>Stylize>Find Edges* to create a coloured outline of your image, then use *Image> Adjustments>Hue/Saturation* to remove the colour by sliding the *Saturation* slider to *-100%*. Finally, change the layer's *Blend Mode* to *Multiply*, allowing the layers to interact.

Workflow tools

✓ TYPE TOOL & FONTS

The font you use will be key to the final appearance of your comic book image. Many websites provide free fonts, such as www.dafont.com and www.1001freefonts. com. The fonts are categorised to help you find the one you want, and often come with category headers, such as 'comic', to make searching easy. Once you've downloaded and installed your free fonts, you can access them from the Character control panel (*Window>Character*). Here, you can control all aspects of typography, including font, size, colour, line, letter spacing and other options. Trying variations of size, colour and weight of the typography can vastly improve the finished comic book image.

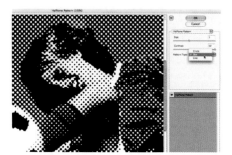

4 Halftone dot pattern Now to add two layers of halftoning to give the effect of old comic book printing. The first is a halftone dot pattern, so duplicate the original image layer, as in step one, then move the layer underneath the pencil outline layer in the Layers palette and go to *Filter> Sketch>Halftone Pattern...* Change the *Pattern Type* to *Dot*, set the *Size* to *5* and *Contrast* to *50*, and click *OK*. Change the *Blend Mode* to *Overlay* and reduce the *Opacity* to *25%*.

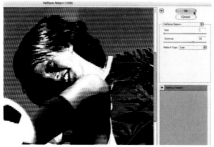

5 Halftone line pattern Duplicate the original image layer once again and move the layer underneath the halftone dot layer in the layer order. Now use *Halftone Pattern* again to put some line details into the shadows of the image. For this, go to *Filter>Sketch>Halftone Pattern...* and enter *Size* as *1* and *Contrast* as *35*, then change *Pattern Type* to *Line* and click *OK*. As with the previous layer, change the *Blend Mode* to *Overlay* and change the *Opacity* to *25%*.

6 Add a border Click on the top layer in the Layers palette and go to *Layer>New>Layer...* to create a new empty layer at the top of the Layers palette. The layer is empty, so to add colour, go to *Edit>Fill* and change *Use* to *White*, and click *OK*. Then change the layer's *Blend Mode* to *Multiply* and the white will become invisible. To add a thick black border, go to *Edit>Stroke...* and enter *20* pixels in *Width*, change *Color* to *Black* and tick *Inside* in the *Location* field, then click *OK*.

7 **Add a caption** Click on the top layer and go to *Layer>New>Layer...* to create another new empty layer at the top of the layer order. Change the *Blend Mode* to *Multiply*, then choose the *Horizontal Type Tool* (inset) and click in the top left-hand corner. Choose a font and size from the *Character* options, then type your caption. If you want another caption at the bottom, simply repeat the steps to create a new layer, then use the *Move Tool* to reposition the text accordingly.

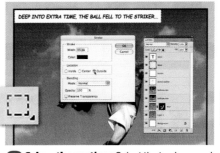

8 **Colour the captions** Select the top layer and go to *Layer>New>Layer...* to create another new empty layer, then move this layer beneath the text layer in the layer order. Using the *Rectangular Marquee Tool* (inset), draw a rectangle selection over the text. Go to *Edit>Fill...* and select *Use* as *White* to fill the selection, then *Edit>Stroke...* at *15* pixels, with *Location* set to *Outside* to create a border. Use the *Move Tool* to tweak position. Repeat this process for the second caption.

9 **Add a speech bubble** Select the top layer; go to *Layer>New>Layer...* to create another new empty layer. Using the *Elliptical Marquee Tool* (inset), draw an oval selection in the desired area of the image. Select the *Polygonal Lasso Tool* and hold *Shift* down to add a point to the oval. Use *Edit>Fill...* and *Edit>Stroke...*, as previously, to colour and border the selection. Create one final new layer above the bubble layer and use the *Type Tool*, as before, to add words to the bubble.

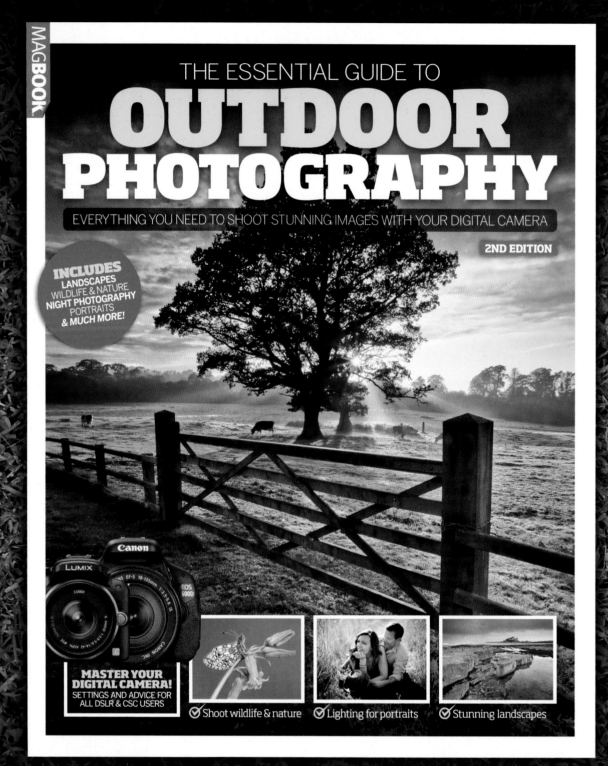

Step-by-step tutorials

PRESENTATION

Add a finishing touch to your images with our favourite ways to present your photos

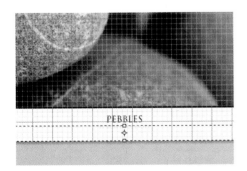

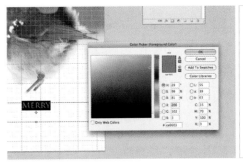

Learn how to frame your prints

Finish off your photographs with a classic framing and title technique

Caroline Wilkinson:
We spend a long time deliberating over how to take our best photographs, but little time considering how to translate them to print. Nowadays, the choices for ways to present your pictures are endless: at-home inkjet prints, speciality lab prints, canvas prints, acrylic prints, art posters or simply just showcased on a website. However you decide to present your images, you should make sure it looks its best and that doesn't stop with Photoshop adjustments. Preparing a picture for output is probably the most overlooked part of post-production but spending a little bit of time framing and titling your image gives it a professional finish and elevates it from a pretty picture to a saleable product. Simply take a look in art stores, or even IKEA, and you'll be hard-pressed not to find a print without these finishing touches. Follow these simple steps to find out how to do it…

☑ TIP: ALTERNATIVE FRAMING

Instead of a white border, why not chose another colour that complements your image. An easy way to change the colour of the border, after you've created it, is to select it using the *Magic Wand Tool*, then using the *Paint Bucket Tool* fill the border with your chosen colour. You may need to change the colour of the *Stroke* border too, as explained in step three.

1 Create the border The first thing to do is add a white frame around the image. Go to *Image>Canvas Size* and add an extra *40mm* to the *Width* and *50mm* to the *Height*. The extra 10mm is to allow room for the text to be added later. Leave the *Anchor* centred, select the *Relative* box and set the *Canvas* extension colour to *White*.

2 Extract the image Select the *Magic Wand Tool* from the toolbar and click on the white border. If part of the image is selected too, decrease the *Tolerance* level in the Options bar. Go to *Select>Inverse* to select the image and then choose *Layer>New>Layer via Cut* to extract the image and paste it on to a new empty layer.

3 Position the image To help with alignment, go to *View>Show>Grid* and then *View>Snap to>Grid*. Using the *Move Tool*, drag the image so the edges are equal width on the top, left and right side – using the grid as a guide. Next, using the *Rectangular Marquee Tool,* select the image, then go to *Edit>Stroke* to add a thin black border. Set the *Width* to *20px*.

4 Add a title Go to *Select>Deselect* to remove the selection and turn off the grid (*View>Show>Grid*) so it is easier to read the text you'll be writing. Using the *Horizontal Type Tool*, create a text box on the white border below the image and type out your title. Use the Options bar to select the text size, type, weight and colour.

PEBBLES
BY ROSS HODDINOTT

5 **Perfect the alignment** Once you're happy with the text, click on the *Center Text* icon in the Options bar to centrally align the text box with the image. Activate the grid lines again to help with this step (*View> Show>Grid*) and using the *Move Tool*, drag the text box over until it snaps to the centre of the image/middle grid line.

6 **Finishing touch** Repeat steps four and five to add a credit line beneath the title. It aesthetically looks better if you make the credit smaller than the title and alter its colour so it's less prominent than the main heading. To change the colour, select the right layer in the Layers palette and click on the coloured box in the Options bar to access the colour picker.

Add a modern grunge frame

Framing a picture is the perfect finishing touch before printing. Find out how to apply unconventional frames for highly creative results

Caroline Wilkinson: Adding a frame to a photograph is really simple: in fact, it took longer to write this article than it did to create the effect. Typically, frames in Photoshop tutorials are plain, straight borders, sometimes with a title added at the bottom: classic, but arguably a little boring for edgier pictures. Grunge borders, on the other hand, add to the character of a photograph and you don't have to create them either – simply blend them with your image. Finding creative frames is fairly easy as you can download many for free or buy certain designs over the internet. There's not much to explain for this tutorial: it's that easy and the results speak for themselves. Pick a frame and give it a go…

Original

Three simple steps to creating a frame

Draw your own Photoshop, especially CS5, has an extensive brush panel (*Window>Brushes*) which features a plethora of brush types and controllable characteristics. One way to create your own border is to draw it on to your picture. It's not the cleanest method and will look rough around the edges, but this can add character to an image. Have a play and see what effects you can create, but we suggest you combine different brush effects and work on an empty layer (*Layer>New Layer*) rather than the image, in case you want to edit or delete the border without affecting the original image.

1 Use the *Rectangular Marquee Tool* to select the inside of your image, leaving the width of the border you want from the edge. Then go to *Select>Inverse* and then *Select>Modify>Feather*, adding a feather of about *20px*.

2 Access the Brushes panel (*Window>Brushes*) and pick your style. We advise making the brush *Diameter* a bit larger than the width of your border so you can create it in a single stroke. Once you're done, go to *Select>Deselect*.

3 The border will probably be fairly clean at this point, which is fine if that's what you want. But if you want to make it look a little grungy, select a brush with *Scattering* and dirty up the edges slightly to get your desired effect.

1 **Open your image** Once you've completed the editing of your image, keep the file open. This type of frame works particularly well on images with a Lomo or vintage toy-camera look, like this one. Now open your chosen frame image and, using the *Move Tool*, drag the image on top of your processed photo. You'll see it automatically creates a new layer.

2 Transform your frame Go to *Edit>Free Transform* and, if you need to rotate your frame, hover the cursor over the corner widget until it bends, then click, hold and rotate. Next, to resize the frame, hold *Shift* to constrain the proportions and drag a corner widget outwards to meet the sides of your image. Press the *Tick* button to commit to the adjustment.

3 Reveal the image Now your frame fits your image, if you want to keep the frame black, change the layer *Blend Mode* to *Multiply* to eliminate any white in the layer, allowing the picture to show through the frame. You could leave it there if you want, but turning the frame white can sometimes add more impact. Go to the next step to see how.

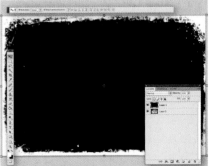

4 Turn it white If you've changed the *Blend Mode* to *Multiply*, change it back to its default *Normal*. Select the frame layer and go to *Layer>Adjustments>Invert* to change it from black to white. Change the *Blend Mode* to *Lighten* to reveal the image. If the centre of your frame layer isn't filled with black or white, there's no need to use a Blend Mode.

How to create a stylish triptych from one image

Get the most from your images using these simple steps to dividing a single shot into three for a creative way of presenting your images

Jordan Butters: Unfortunately fewer and fewer photographers are printing their images and it's such a shame, especially since there are some very creative ways to present pictures these days – with one popular choice being the triptych. In simple terms, a triptych is a series of three images that are either separate pictures linked by a common theme or a single image divided into three sections. It's the latter version we'll show you how to do here. While we've opted to divide our image sections into equal widths, you can make some panels more prominent than others.

There are no rules, only guidelines for how a triptych should look. For instance, if you are creating your triptych from an single photo, consider your choice of image. This finish tends to work best if the original photograph has a point of interest in each section. You can also use images where parts of the scene lead your eye from one panel in to the next, as the curved sea wall does in our example. If your image doesn't have enough interest to divide it into thirds, consider dividing it into two sections for a diptych or four sections for a quadtych using the same technique. Or, rather than a horizontal triptych, make it a vertical sectioning. You can then print them on a single sheet or individually and hang them together. Easy!

Original

HELEN DIXON

1 Create a blank canvas Open your image and go to *Select>All and Edit>Copy*. This not only copies the image, but its dimensions. Create a blank document by going to *File>New*. Leave the dimensions as they are for now and click *OK*. With your blank document open, go to *Image>Canvas Size*. Change the units of measurement from *cm* to *Percent* and change both the *Width* and *Height* to *110*. Click *OK*.

2 Set up the selection tool Open your original image and go to *Select>Deselect Layers*. Pick the *Rectangular Marquee Tool*. Alter the ratio of the rectangle by changing the *Width* to *1* and the *Height* to *2* in the top menu bar. Go to *View>Zoom Out* and zoom out until you can see the full image on screen. Grab the lower right corner of the window and drag it to leave some grey space around your image.

3 Select your first panel Click to the top left of the image, within the grey border, and drag the selection box down past the bottom of the image. Starting and ending your selection outside of the image ensures that you leave no gaps at the top and bottom. This selection will form the first part of your triptych. Go to *Edit>Copy*, open your blank canvas again and go to *Edit>Paste*. The first part of your triptych will appear in the centre.

Final image
As a finishing touch, add a shadow by clicking on the *Add a layer style* button in the Layers palette and selecting *Drop Shadow*. Repeat for each layer.

4 Add the other panels Head back over to your image and select the next panel, starting your selection from the top right of your current selection and dragging down to the bottom of the image again. Go to *Edit>Copy*, open your canvas again and go to *Edit>Paste*. Repeat this step for the final part of your image. All three parts of your triptych will be stacked on top of each other on the blank canvas, so it's time to space them out.

5 Space out the images Close your main image without saving and work on your new canvas. Making sure that *Layer 1* is selected in the Layers palette, select the *Move Tool*. Hold down the *Shift* key, and click and drag the layer to the left until it locks on to the side of the other layers. Select *Layer 3* in the Layers palette and repeat, this time dragging to the right until it locks into place. It will look similar to your original image.

6 Create borders With Layer 3 still selected, hold down the *Shift* key again and tap the *Right Arrow* key to create a border. Count the number of times you tap the key. Select *Layer 1* in the Layers palette and, holding down the *Shift* key again, tap the *Left Arrow* key an equal number of times to create an equal-size gap on the other side. Holding down the *Shift* key moves your image five pixels at a time.

Original

ROSS HODDINOTT

Create your own photo Christmas cards

Dust off your inkjet printer and invest in quality card and envelopes so you can send friends and family greetings cards with a personal touch this Christmas. This very simple step-by-step will show you how...

Caroline Wilkinson: It's safe to say most of us will be sending out a few family Christmas cards this year, but instead of buying them why not create your own? We're not talking about using lots of Pritt Stick and glitter, but rather cards that showcase some of your most beautiful winter or festive imagery, or even a family portrait. It probably won't work out as cheap as buying cliché cards in bulk, but it will give friends and family something unique and special enough that it will probably be the only card to survive the post-Christmas clear out!

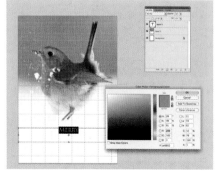

1 Create a blank card Click *File>New*, then *Preset*: *International Paper* and *Size*: *A5*. Make sure *Color Mode* is *RGB Color* before clicking *OK*. Now open your image and, using the *Move Tool*, click and drag it on to your canvas. If you need to resize it to fit, use the *Move Tool* holding down *Shift* to constrain the proportions.

2 Add text Turn the grid on to use as a guide (*View>Show>Grid*) and then create a text box using the *Type Tool*. Type out your greeting and then double-click the words to highlight them: you can now experiment with type and size. For colour, click on the swatches at the bottom of the toolbar to open the colour palette.

3 Apply a border Now add an inset border by selecting the *Rectangular Marquee Tool* and drawing a frame within your image. Then go to *Edit>Stroke* and click *Inside*, set the *Width* to *5px* and click on the colour swatch to select your border colour. Click *OK*. To turn off the grid go *View>Show>Grid*.

Merry *Christmas*

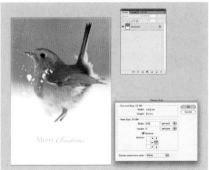

4 **Edit any elements** If you want to go back to edit the text at any point, simply click on the **Text** layer in the Layers palette and use the **Type Tool** to select the text again. Here we changed the colour to match the border and combined two different fonts for extra interest: Bickham Script Pro and Minion Pro.

5 **Extend canvas** In preparation for print, flatten the file (*Layer>Flatten Image*) and enlarge the canvas to **A4** by selecting *Image>Canvas Size*. Under **New Size** change **cm** to **percent**, set **Width** to **100** and change the **Anchor** point by clicking on the middle right anchor to set the image to the right-hand side.

6 **Get ready to print** To finish it off, add your website address and name to the back of the card using the same method as in step two. Then, to get the card ready for print, go to *File>Print* and select *Scale to Fit Media,* then the type of paper you're using and set print **Quality** to **Maximum** for the best possible results. Now print away!

Useful Photoshop shortcuts for PC & Mac

General	PC-Windows	Apple Mac
New file	<Ctrl> N	<Cmd> N
Open file	<Ctrl> O	<Cmd> O
Close file	<Ctrl> W	<Cmd> W
Save file	<Ctrl> S	<Cmd> S
Save file as	<Shift> <Ctrl> S	<Shift> <Cmd> S
Print file	<Ctrl> P	<Cmd> P
Step backward (undo)	<Ctrl> Z	<Cmd> Z
Step forward (redo)	<Ctrl> Y	<Cmd> Y
Free Transform	<Ctrl> T	<Cmd> T
Apply Transform	<enter>	<return>
Copy selection	<Ctrl> C	<Cmd> C
Cut selection	<Ctrl> X	<Cmd> X
Paste selection as new layer	<Ctrl> V	<Cmd> V
Image size	<Alt> <Ctrl> I	<option> <Cmd> S
Levels	<Ctrl> L	<Cmd> L
Select default colours	D	D
Swap background / foreground colours	X	X
Repeat last filter used	<Ctrl> F	<Cmd> F
Adjust Hue / Saturation	<Ctrl> U	<Cmd> U
Show / hide rulers	<Shift> <Ctrl> R	<Shift> <Cmd> R
Toggle Quick Mask mode	Q	Q

Auto Adjustments	PC-Windows	Apple Mac
Auto Smart Fix	<Alt> <Ctrl> M	<option> <Cmd> M
Auto Levels	<Shift> <Ctrl> L	<Shift> <Cmd> L
Auto Contrast	<Alt> <Shift> <Ctrl> L	<option> <Shift> <Cmd> L
Auto colour	<Shift> <Ctrl> B	<Shift> <Cmd> B
Auto red-eye fix	<Ctrl> R	<Cmd> R

Selections	PC-Windows	Apple Mac
Select all	<Ctrl> A	<Cmd> A
Deselect	<Ctrl> D	<Cmd> D
Invert selection	<Shift> <Ctrl> I	<Shift> <Cmd> I
Feather selection	<Alt> <Ctrl> D	<option> <Cmd> D
Add to selection	<Shift> and selection tool	<Shift> and selection tool
Remove from selection	<Alt> and selection tool	<option> and selection tool
Show / hide selection boundary	<Ctrl> H	<Cmd> H
Constrain marquee (circle or square)	<Shift> and shape tool	<Shift> and shape tool
Draw marquee from centre	<Alt> and shape tool	<option> and shape tool
Exit crop tool	<esc>	<esc>

Layers	PC-Windows	Apple Mac
New Layer	<Shift> <Ctrl> N	<Shift> <Cmd> N
Copy Layer	<Ctrl> J	<Cmd> J
Group layers	<Ctrl> G	<Cmd> G
Ungroup layers	<Shift> <Ctrl> G	<Shift> <Cmd> G
Merge layers	<Ctrl> E	<Cmd> E
Merge all visible layers	<Shift> <Ctrl> E	<Shift> <Cmd> E

Zooming	PC-Windows	Apple Mac
Zoom in	<Ctrl> +	<Cmd> +
Zoom out	<Ctrl> –	<Cmd> –
Fit on screen	<Ctrl> 0	<Cmd> 0
Actual pixels (100% zoom)	<Alt> <Ctrl> 0	<option> <Cmd> 0
Scroll using hand tool	<spacebar> use mouse	<spacebar> use mouse

Drawing tools	PC-Windows	Apple Mac
Eye dropper	<Alt> in painting or shape tool	<option> in painting or shape tool
Fill with background colour	<Ctrl> <backspace>	<Cmd> <delete>
Increase brush size	]	]
Decrease brush size	[	[
Increase brush hardness	<Shift>]	<Shift>]
Decrease brush hardness	<Shift> [	<Shift> [